A SAVORY HISTORY OF ARKANSAS DELTA FOOD

POTLIKKER, COON SUPPERS & CHOCOLATE GRAVY

CINDY GRISHAM

AMERICAN PALATE

Published by American Palate
A Division of The History Press
Charleston, SC 29403
www.historypress.net

All photographs by author unless otherwise noted.

First published 2013

Manufactured in the United States

ISBN 978.1.60949.980.8

Library of Congress Cataloging-in-Publication Data

Grisham, Cindy.
A savory history of Arkansas Delta food : pot likker, coon suppers and chocolate gravy / Cindy Grisham.
pages cm
Includes bibliographical references and index.
ISBN 978-1-60949-980-8
1. Food--Arkansas--Arkansas Delta--History. 2. Food habits--Arkansas--Arkansas Delta--History. 3. Cooking, American--Southern style. 4. Cooking--Arkansas--Arkansas Delta. 5. Arkansas Delta (Ark.)--Social life and customs. 6. Oral history--Arkansas--Arkansas Delta. 7. Arkansas Delta (Ark.)--Biography. I. Title.
TX360.U62A754 2013
641.59767--dc23
2013016428

CONTENTS

CHAPTER 1

THE OTHER DELTA

On ground so flat and low and marshy, lies a breeding-place of fever, ague, and death…a dismal swamp…teeming with rank, unwholesome vegetation…a jungle deep and dark, with neither earth nor water at its roots, but putrid matter, formed of the pulpy offal of the two, and of their corruption.[1]

—Charles Dickens, American Notes *(1842)*

This is a story about food. Specifically, it is about the history and culture of food in the northeast corner of the state of Arkansas, an area not usually known for its cuisine. Then again, it isn't well known at all. The idea for it was born over a plate of biscuits and gravy on what my friends and I called Biscuits and Gravy Tuesday, which I will discuss in greater detail later on. Those afternoon conversations about our memories of food and family tended to drag on long after we had returned to work and grew to include many other friends and acquaintances. I learned long ago that people never grow tired of talking about the food they love and the people they love who cooked it for them. There is much to tell.

Northeast Arkansas lies in an area known as the Arkansas Delta (known locally as just "the Delta"), which is basically the same as the Delta over in Mississippi, except nobody knows as much about it. In 1935, a historian named David Cohn asserted that the Delta "begins in the lobby of the Peabody Hotel in Memphis and ends on Catfish Row in Vicksburg."[2] Cohn's description has shaped the image of the region in the hearts and minds of a nation and the world, but it narrowed their vision of it as well. The Delta is as much a state of mind as it is a place, and it extends far beyond a few counties in northwest Mississippi. To understand the place better, you have to have a short lesson in geography and geology and history. It can't be helped, so here it goes.

The Delta is not actually a delta at all but rather an alluvial plain—the Mississippi River Alluvial Plain to be exact. An alluvial plain is nothing more than a flat piece of land that was formed by sediments left lying around after floods, which means that most of the Delta used to be someplace else. This Mississippi River Alluvial Plain is subdivided into three smaller regions. The first is the well-known area called the Mississippi Delta. Now, it really is a delta, although not of the Mississippi but of one of its tributaries, the Yazoo. The center of this region is Greenville, Mississippi, a town that calls itself "the Heart and Soul of the Delta." Greenville is known for its writers and historians. People like William Alexander Percy, who's *Lanterns on the Levee: Recollections of a Planter's Son* sets the stage for the Delta as most of us know it, or Shelby Foote, the historian of the Civil War.[3]

The second region is called the Mississippi River Delta and lies in southern Louisiana. It actually is the real delta of the Mississippi. The heart of this region is New Orleans, a city well known for its quirky charm, beautiful architecture and good times. The third part of the plain is called the Mississippi Embayment. It takes in a little tiny corner of northeastern Louisiana, all of eastern Arkansas and the extreme southeastern corner of Missouri. The heart of the embayment is Memphis, which in spite of its metropolitan identity is still just a big old country town. The lower part of the embayment is historically similar to the Mississippi Delta on the other side of the river. The land was settled before the Civil War, with large sections of timbered land cleared by slaves, who later toiled there to grow cotton. The upper part was settled much later and because of that has a history and culture that, though similar to the rest of the Delta, is a world all its own.

Within the Mississippi Embayment, there are smaller areas—three to be exact—that need to be explained as well. The first is Crowley's Ridge, a geological oddity that pushes up out of the flat farmland that surrounds it. Known locally as "the Ridge," it rises from 250 to 550 feet above the alluvial plain, stretches from 0.5 to 12.0 miles in width and runs for 150.0 miles from a point in southeast Missouri directly across the river from a town called Thebes, Illinois, all the way to the Mississippi River town of Helena in Phillips County, Arkansas. It is covered with a soil called loess, which means that it was deposited by the winds rather than the water. If you spend much time in the Delta, you will quickly understand how the wind could have left all that dirt. No one can agree on its origin, with some believing that it was

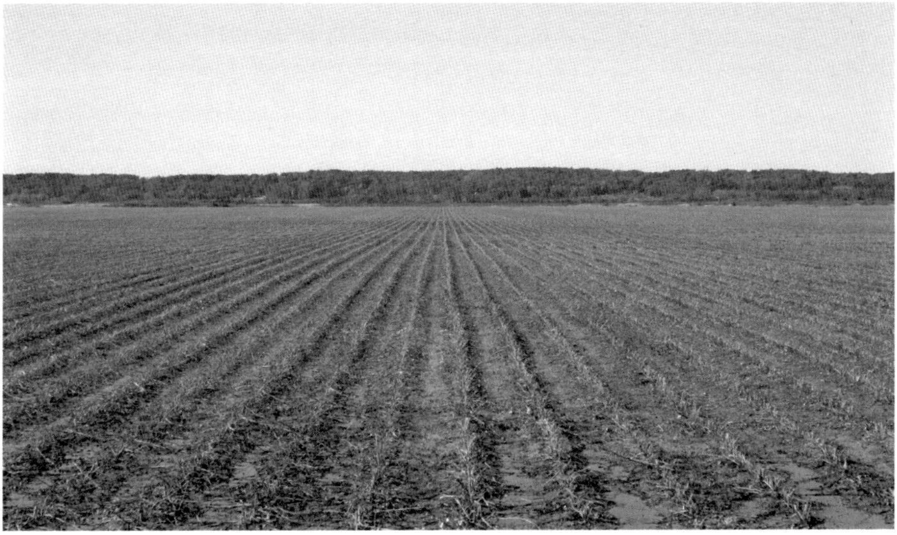

Looking across a cotton field toward Crowley's Ridge, near Weona in Poinsett County.

the land between the old beds of the Mississippi and Ohio Rivers and others thinking that it may have been pushed up by the New Madrid Seismic Zone, which lies underneath and has from time to time caused a great deal of trouble. The plants and animals that inhabit the Ridge are strangely similar to those in the Appalachian Mountains. Because it was high land, above the flooding of the lowlands surrounding it, the Ridge was the first place settled in the region.

On the western side of the Ridge lie the Western Lowlands, whose sediments come primarily from the White River but also from streams with names like the Cache, the L'Anguille and Bayou de View. It is low and swampy but fertile, and it is here where much of the world's rice is grown. On the eastern side of Crowley's Ridge lies the Eastern Lowlands. There, the sediments come not only from the Mississippi River but also from the St. Francis, Little and Tyronza Rivers. This has historically been the cotton growing region.

Arkansas has often seemed to be at the wrong place at the wrong time, with its geography primarily to blame. Although it lies right across the Mississippi River and would have been one of the first places new settlers would have entered going west, the swampy lands on the eastern side were so difficult to cross that most people went north to Missouri or south to Louisiana, where travel was easier. Roads were next to impossible to construct, and although the terrain was crisscrossed with rivers and bayous, they were only navigable part of the year. In 1822, Congress appropriated money to construct a federal highway, a military road from the Mississippi River near Memphis to Little Rock, and appropriated $26,000 to complete the project, a fairly princely sum at that time. It took the entire amount just to cross Crittenden County, and the officer in charge begged to go to some nice northern climate.[4]

Northeast Arkansas is sometimes referred to as the "final frontier," and in many ways it was, for it was the last part of the lower forty-eight states to open up and develop. A series of large earthquakes rocked the area during the winter of 1811–12, and what few settlers there were in many cases fled to a safer location. The land itself was changed drastically, and in many places, it literally sank many feet and filled with water. The St. Francis River channel was partially destroyed by the quakes, leaving most of the Eastern Lowlands completely or partially covered with water most of the year. The place was a veritable hunter's paradise but was next to impossible to clear and settle. Without humans to clear the land and with fertile soils and abundant water, northeast Arkansas became a verdant, thick forest teeming with plant and animal life, yet tangled and dark. It was what one scholar of the region called "a seething, lush hell."[5] The great stands of timber that towered above the primeval swamps were coveted by timber men in the North and Midwest, as well as by the railroads, which needed it to build towns and power steam engines in the Far West. Determined to conquer the swamps and take out the timber, the railroad began work in northeast Arkansas in the early 1880s, and great hordes of men seeking work poured into the area from all over the country. Men are always followed by women and children, and by 1900, there were finally signs of civilization in the region. It was a rough civilization, but a civilization nonetheless.

Once the timber was gone, people in the region realized the value of the soil, and farming began on the cleared tracts of land. Cotton was king in the Delta during the early part of the twentieth century, and settlers moved into the region to make their fortunes. Cotton is a fickle mistress, however, and the majority of these farmers failed in their endeavor, losing their land to the furnishing merchants in the small towns. The merchants were schooled in the art of business and not agriculture, and they needed farmers to tend their ever-growing tracts of land. Settlers in the form of sharecroppers and tenant farmers, both black and white, moved into the region to try their hands at farming the fertile soils. As the small farm towns grew along the railroad, they attracted new people to the region, including Italian, Chinese and Mediterranean immigrants, as well as a small Jewish population primarily

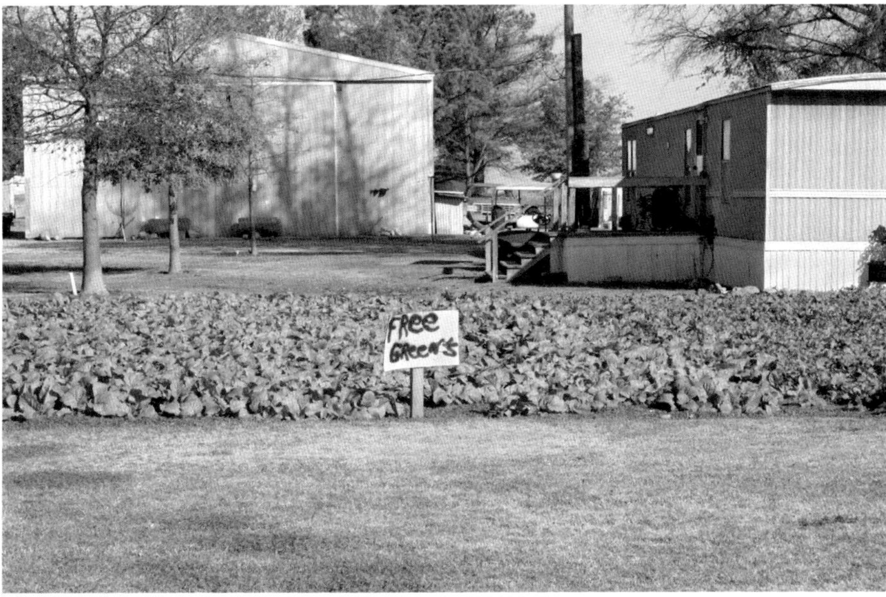

Greens patch near Bowman in Craighead County. It is not uncommon in the Delta to see patches like this in gardens and fields with handmade signs offering "free greens." It is a sign of the cooperative spirit that makes the Delta a wonderful place to live.

from eastern Europe. All brought new ways of eating and cooking to the Delta. By the mid-1950s, changes in agriculture had forced the sharecroppers out, and they were replaced by day labor in the form of Mexican nationals from a federal work program known as the Bracero Program. Again, new foods arrived in the Delta, forever changing the eating habits of those who live here. The result of all this cultural mishmash is a creative cuisine that is at once common yet unique.

We will begin our journey to experience and understand the food of northeast Arkansas' Delta region. Along the way, we will visit lifelong residents both young and old and enjoy meals in small-town diners and cafés and at roadside barbecue stands. We'll talk to up-and-coming young farmers, beekeepers and just plain folks who plant extra turnips in the fall to share with anyone who might want or need them. We have had conversations with black folks and white folks and every shade in the middle of those who call this place home. We'll begin our journey now. You're welcome to come along.

CHAPTER 2

THE NATURAL STATE OF FOOD

Food was important, though: food for a long winter, one that would follow a bad crop, one in which everything we ate would come from the garden. There was nothing unusual about this, except that there wouldn't be a spare dime to buy anything but flour, sugar, and coffee. A good crop meant there was a little money tucked away under a mattress, a few bills rolled up and saved and sometimes used for luxuries like Coca-Cola's, ice cream, saltines, and white bread. A bad crop meant that if we didn't grow it, we didn't eat.[6]

–*John Grisham,* A Painted House

This whole book started over a plate of biscuits and gravy. Every Tuesday afternoon at 2:00 p.m., following our graduate-level class in Southern Politics at Arkansas State University, my friends Bradley George and Sarah Sisney would join me in a plate of biscuits and gravy at a little restaurant in Jonesboro, Arkansas, called H.T. Ponder's. We loved H.T. Ponder's because it was not a chain, and you could get breakfast anytime the doors were open. For me and Bradley, gravy was that thick, lovely, creamy white goo made from sausage or bacon drippings and milk, seasoned with salt and black pepper. For Sarah, it was a concoction called chocolate gravy, which I had never even heard of before moving to the Arkansas Delta. She enjoyed it immensely, claiming that it was the only chocolate gravy she had ever found that tasted just like her mother's. It was thick and custardy whereas, she claimed, most restaurant chocolate gravy was thin and syrupy. It looked and tasted like chocolate pudding. To me, whether it was thin and syrupy or thick and custardy, it seemed like a waste of a good biscuit. To Sarah, it was pure nirvana.

In addition to the eating on those Tuesday afternoons, there was a never-ending discussion of food brought on by that gravy. Where did the recipe come from? When did you eat it? What did you eat with it? Oftentimes, those conversations would continue back on campus, where we were joined by students and faculty alike in discussions about their grandmas' cathead biscuits and the proper method for making chicken and dumplings. At Bradley's house, Christmas was just not Christmas without a big bowl of chicken and dumplings alongside the more common holiday dishes. Those dumplings were of a light and fluffy variety, made by dropping a sticky ball of dough from a spoon into a boiling pot of seasoned broth. At our friend Christy's house, they had to be of a sturdier variety, the dough stiff and rolled out on a board, cut into strips or squares and then dropped in the broth. It really didn't matter how the broth was prepared as long as the dumplings were of the right variety.

A couple of years down the road, I was working as a graduate assistant at the Southern Tenant Farmers Museum in Tyronza, Arkansas, and our museum store had just began stocking some products bearing the new designation "Arkansas Delta Made."[7] One of those products was a can of Granny Clay's Chocolate Gravy mix created by a wonderful woman from the town of Marked Tree named Regina Clay. It was the same gravy she had grown up eating and had fed to her children, and she wanted to share that with the rest of the world. That gravy mix sparked more conversations than possibly anything else in the building. Unless they were from Arkansas, they generally had not heard of chocolate gravy either. I started talking to a lot of native Arkansans about their memories of food—what they grew up eating in their grandmother's kitchen, their holiday traditions and even funeral traditions because, in the South, mourning brings people together, and wherever they gather, they are going to eat.

Since I know you are dying to make some chocolate gravy of your own, here is a recipe from *The Museum Cookbook*, compiled by the ladies of Marked Tree (Poinsett County). This one uses water instead of milk and produces a nice sauce with a creamy consistency. Traditionally, it is served as a breakfast food over hot biscuits that have been buttered before the gravy is poured over them. If you are watching fat, skip the butter; it is just as

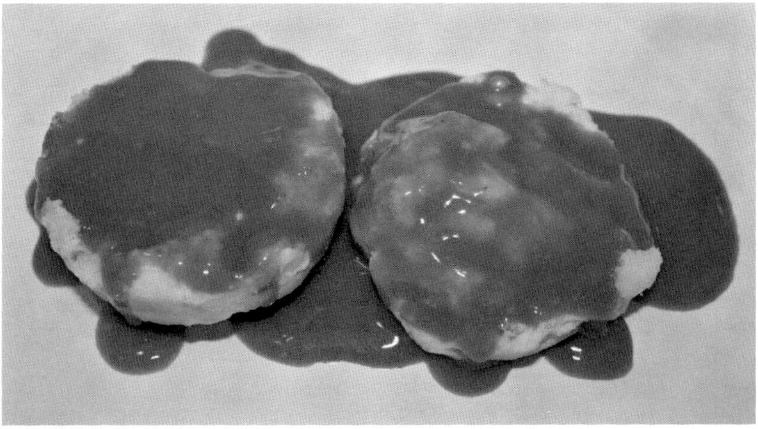

A plate of biscuits with a helping of chocolate gravy, a breakfast staple in the Arkansas Delta.

good on plain biscuits. It would also make a good dessert. If you would rather buy Granny Clay's mix instead of making it yourself, the contact information is in the appendix at the back of the book.

CHOCOLATE GRAVY

3 cups boiling water
1 heaping tablespoon cocoa
2 heaping tablespoons flour
1 dash salt
½ to ¾ cup sugar (according to how sweet you like it)

Bring water to a boil and keep it boiling. Mix all dry ingredients and sift together to make certain there are no lumps. Pour dry ingredients in a saucepan on high heat. Pour in one cup of boiling water and stir. Continue adding boiling water until the gravy is the thickness desired. Boil for three minutes, stirring constantly. This should be a very smooth sauce. Pour over hot biscuits.

Ask the average American what he or she knows about Arkansas, and you will get a blank stare. It sits smack dab in the middle of the country, hiding in plain sight. Arkansas is a daughter of the Old Confederacy and was the seventh state to secede and cast its lot with the Lost Cause. Poor Arkansas was just about as popular then as now—when the Confederates were faced with the proposition of losing Tennessee or hanging on to Arkansas, they chose Tennessee. They took the Arkansas men who would join the army, moved them out of the state militia and into the Confederate army, sent them east to fight and then abandoned everyone else to just hang on and do the best they could do. Arkansas had been doing fairly well economically before the war—Crittenden, Phillips, Arkansas, Desha and Chicot Counties were among the thirty-six richest counties in the country when the war began.[8] The devastation afterward was so severe that the state has yet to truly recover. Arkansas was also the gateway to the Southwest, with Fort Smith serving as the seat of government for the Indian Territory, but these days, the West will not claim it either. We just fly along under everyone else's radar most of the time, and that suits most of the residents just fine.

I have a good friend who says that Arkansas should be billed as the "Best Small Town in America," for it truly seems like one big small town. Ranked by landmass, it is twenty-ninth in size, with just over 53,000 square miles of land. Fewer than 3 million people call the state home, though, most living in rural areas where everyone knows everyone else. The largest city is Little Rock, with fewer than 200,000 people spread out over a landmass of 116 square miles. The people are friendly, the cost of living is low and it is altogether a pretty nice place to call home. Politicians must cover every inch of the state to get themselves elected, so we know our governors and senators fairly well. Everyone seems to know everyone else personally, or at least roomed with their cousin at college. Because of that closeness, there is a desire to share food and conversation when we gather. History tells us that even the earliest-known Arkansans were generous with their foodstuffs. Yes, it's time for another history lesson.

The first written reports of food in Arkansas come from the year 1541. It was then, on June 28, that Hernando de Soto and several hundred of his soldiers crossed what they called the Great River into present-day Arkansas and became the first Europeans to see the place. Rodrigo Ranjel, Luys Hernández de Biedma and an unnamed Portuguese soldier known only to this day as the "Gentleman of Elvas" kept journals of the trip, chronicling the people they met, the villages they encountered and the food that was shared with them by the native people of the Mississippian culture.[9] Of course, being a good host does not mean that you will not be attacked, your homes burned and your storehouses looted, all of which unfortunately occurred a great deal of the time.

The Mississippians were the last prehistoric culture before the arrival of the Europeans, arising in about AD 800. Like today, there were several regional variations of Mississippian culture, with our eastern Arkansas people forming part of the Middle Mississippians, who were centered on the central Mississippi Valley, lower Ohio Valley and the majority of the mid-South region, including northern Alabama and Mississippi, western Tennessee and western and central Kentucky. The people lived in residential complexes with large ceremonial platform mounds, their towns usually surrounded by moats and palisade walls. They were excellent artisans and craftsmen, and many examples of their ceramic creations, both decorative and utilitarian, survive in the finest museums in the country (most of them outside the boundaries of Arkansas because the looting did not stop after the people were gone).

Outside the walls of the towns lay extensive agricultural fields, generally tended and watched over by the women and consisting of maize, beans, squash and assorted seed and grain crops. The people were also hunters, eating venison, bear, raccoon, opossum and a wide variety of birds and waterfowl that traveled through the area along the Great Mississippi Flyway. The moats, while an excellent security measure against enemies, also contained an outstanding assortment of delicious fish such as catfish and buffalo fish, as well as turtles and frogs. Pecans are first noted by the Spanish at the paramount village of the chiefdom of Casqui, as well as two different kinds of persimmons and other fruits.

Casqui is believed by most scholars to be the Parkin site in eastern Cross County and lies within the boundaries of the present-day Parkin Archaeological State Park. The large ceremonial mound, although greatly reduced in size over the years, is still an impressive thing to behold. The village complex is composed of a seventeen-acre raised "tell," surrounded on three sides by a moat that is still visible and on the fourth by the St. Francis River. Pecans still grow at the site, as do walnuts, persimmons, wild grapes, passion fruit and other native foods. The Spanish, for their part, contributed a new animal into the local environment in the form of pigs, which they had brought with them on the journey as food on the hoof. The pigs were easy to transport, and they multiplied rapidly, keeping the Spaniards in meat, but pigs being pigs, a few managed to escape into the surrounding forests, where they still exist in many parts of the state today. We probably have De Soto to thank for the University of Arkansas' mascot, the Razorback. Woo Pig Sooie.

De Soto and his crew wandered around Arkansas for almost a year, causing mayhem wherever they went. They never found the gold and riches they were seeking and grew increasingly disillusioned. By the time De Soto sent an exploratory party down the Mississippi River seeking the Gulf of Mexico, his forces were down to half of the original number. De Soto contracted a fever and died on May 31, 1542, near modern-day Lake Village, Arkansas. Since he had convinced the Indians that he was a god, calling himself the "Son of the Sun," his men were forced to weight down his body and dump it in the Mississippi under cover of darkness because they feared that once the Indians realized they had been tricked about De Soto's mortality, their lives would be at risk. The remaining soldiers eventually built new boats and floated down the river to the Gulf and back toward home in 1543.[10]

The next Europeans to come to Arkansas, the Frenchmen Father Jacques Marquette and fur trader Louis Joliet, arrived in June 1673. There was no sign of the Mississippian villages or the people in northeast Arkansas, and their fate remains unknown to this day. The duo did find another group of Indians along the Arkansas River in present-day Desha County in southeast Arkansas, a group calling themselves the Quapaws. The Quapaws were not only a handsome people but were friendly as well, and the explorers were treated to much feasting of the same sort of food that De Soto had been provided when he came through the area. The Frenchmen called the Quapaws the Arkansas, which was their mangled pronunciation of another Native American word, *arcansa*, which translates to either "downstream people" or "people of the south wind." Whichever, the name stuck, and Arkansas it has remained. Interestingly enough, the pronunciation of Arkansas is a modern mangling of the original French mangling, which was eventually established by state law in 1881. Torn over what the correct form of the name was, the pronunciation "*ar*-kan-saw" won out over the one that rhymed with Kansas. Note that the river bearing the same name, which flows across the state from west to east and joins the Mississippi in the southeast part of the state, is pronounced "ar-*kan*-zəs" everywhere but Arkansas.

The French remained as well, or at least they came back pretty quickly, establishing the first European outpost in the state, the Post of Arkansas,[11] now better known as Arkansas Post, at the intersection of the Arkansas and Mississippi Rivers in 1686. It consisted of a hut and six men, but the Quapaws supported it, and the little village flourished. The French developed a taste for Quapaw food, especially smoked buffalo tongue, and salted tongue became one of the major exports of the state. The Quapaws developed a taste for European fruit, especially the peach, and trees were planted extensively in the area. It was at the post that Arkansas' first-known barbecue cook practiced her art, a woman known up and down the rivers for her excellent flair for cooking meat. Hers is a story worthy of its own book.[12]

By the beginning of the nineteenth century, people were beginning to enter into the territory that now belonged to the United States, and while everyone knows about Lewis and Clark and their foray across the newly acquired lands, most are unaware that there were other surveys as well. One of those was undertaken by two men, Dr. George Hunter and William Dunbar, who came into what is now northern Louisiana and southern Arkansas, exploring the Ouachita (pronounced "*wash*-a-tah") River and the beautiful land that lay around it. While not as extensive as the trip undertaken by Lewis and Clark, it was notable for being more purely scientific.[13] The American people now knew of what was to become Arkansas and began to enter the territory. A natural disaster, though, slowed the growth and changed the Delta region of northeast Arkansas forever.

In the early morning hours of December 16, 1811, the land along what is now known as the New Madrid Seismic Zone shifted violently. For the next three months, the ground rarely stopped shaking. Eyewitness accounts tell of the land rolling like the ocean literally for days at a time. Lowlands rose up and forests sunk down, and by the time it was over, those who had not fled out of fear were left in a place that in many ways no longer resembled their old home. River channels were rerouted or even completely destroyed, and the land was left a tangled mass of swamp. The American government later issued War of 1812 bounty land certificates in northeast Arkansas to veterans of the conflict as partial payment for their services but had to rescind them in many cases because the land was deemed unlivable at the time.[14]

Because the valley of the St. Francis River in northeast Arkansas had been so changed by the earthquakes, it became known as the St. Francis Sunk Lands. For a major part of the nineteenth century, the Sunk Lands were the exclusive domain of men who made their way fishing, hunting and trapping. The only real growth lay along the highland that split the region in half, called Crowley's Ridge. The few people from the outside to come into the Arkansas Delta tended to be educated men from the Northeast or foreign scholars and travelers from Europe. Like most travel writers, they told the stories of the unique and unusual so that most of the things related about the state resemble a modern reality television show—men like

George Featherstonhaugh (believe it or not, that last name is pronounced "Fenshaw"), a British geologist sent to the Arkansas territory in 1834 and 1835 to produce a geological survey, and Edward Palmer, a botanist sent out by the Smithsonian to study the Native American mounds in the 1880s. Unaccustomed to a frontier way of life, they noted the extremes in their reports. It makes for entertaining reading, but it probably was not the normal way of life for most of the settlers.[15]

The push to settle the Far West brought a need for timber to build railroads, towns and homes. The Sunk Lands had remained uncut and contained some of the largest hardwood forests in the nation. The railroads realized that if they could penetrate the Sunk Lands, they would have access to the riches that lay there. So, in the 1880s, they began making their way through, building up the rail beds on high levees to stay above water; the clearing began. Railroaders, followed by lumbermen and entrepreneurs of all kinds, poured into the region, and the last great wilderness succumbed, leaving a rich, deep, fertile soil that could grow anything, including that great maker or breaker of man, cotton.

Cotton succeeded in breaking most of them, but the ones who made it truly made it big. As the land reverted back to farms again, like it had been with the Mississippians, it filled with the people needed to grow and tend the crops. While the Indians had been communal in their agriculture, modern Americans were individualists who wanted to make their own way. The flatlands filled up so that every twenty to forty acres, there was a family living and working the land. Mechanization came slowly to Arkansas, but it came just the same, and the land once full of families and homes emptied out, leaving nothing but the small towns and the crops. This is the story of the people who lived through these turbulent times, told through the food they ate and still enjoy.

Let me say that this is not an academic history of the foodways of the Delta people, for that would take far too long to complete the in-depth study it would require and to compile the findings, although it is a worthy effort that needs to be tackled. It is instead a lighthearted look at a regional cuisine. Before you laugh at my calling the food of the Arkansas Delta "cuisine," remember that the word simply means a way of preparing food, so there is a Delta cuisine. It is primarily southern, with hints of the Midwest and the Southwest and with an occasional international twist as well, for in a boomtown, everyone comes to make their fortune. The only restaurant in tiny Crawfordsville, Arkansas, is Italian, operated by the descendants of immigrants brought to the state to work as sharecroppers, although they are as famous for their catfish and barbecue as for their pasta. Every little town had what was always referred to as the "Chinaman's Store," operated by a Cantonese immigrant whose descendants are still here somewhere. In tiny Joiner, Arkansas, during the Great Depression, the entire business district was either eastern European Jews or Lebanese. It is also a cuisine based on the agricultural traditions of the Native Americans, who built an advanced civilization on this land before the Europeans came, bringing their customs and tastes, and later enhanced by the African slaves and their descendants who came to sharecrop. It is not high and fancy food but rather good, simple, hearty fare, and like most regional cuisines, you either love it or hate it. I hope you enjoy learning about it.[16]

CHAPTER 3
MOTHER CORN AND HER SISTERS

My name is Charlie Brennan, from Charlestown I come.
I've traveled this wide world over, and many a race I've run,
I've traveled this wide world over, and some ups and downs I saw,
But I never knew what mis'ry was till I came to Arkansas.

I followed my conductor to his respected place,
Where pity and starvation was seen in every face.
His bread it was corn dodger, his meat I could not chaw,
But he charged me half a dollar in the state of Arkansas.

O now I am a railroad man at a dollar and a half a day.
An' there I 'low to work, boys, till I can get away,
Then I'll go to the Cherokee mountains and marry me a squaw,
Farewell to hog and hominy in the state of Arkansas.[17]
—*"The State of Arkansas,"* Folksongs of North America

Although northeast Arkansas seems like a young country, most of its communities being only around one hundred years old, it was the center of a vibrant civilization for centuries before that. The Middle Mississippian culture covered the state in the days before the Europeans arrived. They were an agricultural people, growing fields of crops around their villages. By saving and planting seeds from the fruits, vegetables and grains that were large and tasted the best, they improved the crops, making their fields more productive and the food from them healthier. Some scientists even believe that the central United States, particularly Missouri and Arkansas, might have been the site of domestication of some varieties of squash (*Curcubita pepo*) that originated from the wild gourd of the Ozarks, a pesky little vine that still grows along the rivers here.[18]

In spite of what we have always learned from the movies, Indians did not all live on buffalo. The ancient people of northeast Arkansas had a wide and varied diet that still affects the way we eat here today. They cultivated protein-rich seeds like sunflower, which they not only ate plain but also ground into flours to make breads and to thicken soups and stews. The De Soto expedition reported that villages in the region were surrounded by fruit and nut trees that grew in orchards and seemed to have been picked out by the villagers to save and protect—things like persimmon, wild plums and an assortment of nuts and berries. The most important crops, though, were those that continue to form the center of the regional diet to this day: corn, beans and squash.

They are called the Three Sisters[19] by the Indians because of their interdependent growing habits and because of the way they should be eaten together. Corn, or maize, is the base crop. It is planted first and allowed to reach a height of about six inches. At this point, beans are planted beside the corn plants. They will sprout and twine themselves around the tall cornstalks, using them as a trellis of sorts. Finally, the squashes are planted between the hills. They grow up and surround the other two plants. The squash acts as a shade for the ground, keeping the soil temperatures down and the sun off of the soil, which helps it retain moisture. They also shade the weeds, which keeps them from sprouting as often and, for those that do sprout, from growing as quickly. This allows as much of the nutrients and water as possible to go to the food plants. The corn was eaten fresh in the summer the way we usually enjoy it today, on the cob. A second crop would then be planted, and this one would be allowed to dry on the stalk for later use. Beans could be eaten fresh, either as snap beans or fresh shelled beans, or they could be dried on the vine and shelled out for use later on. The squash was at first used only for the protein-rich seeds, but as the Indians worked to improve the plant, thicker rinds with more flavorful flesh were created, and these began to be used as well. It could be used fresh or cut into rings and hung over the fires on sticks to dry for winter use.

Corn has been the primary staple of people in the southern United States for centuries. Today, we use it mainly in what the Indians called the green

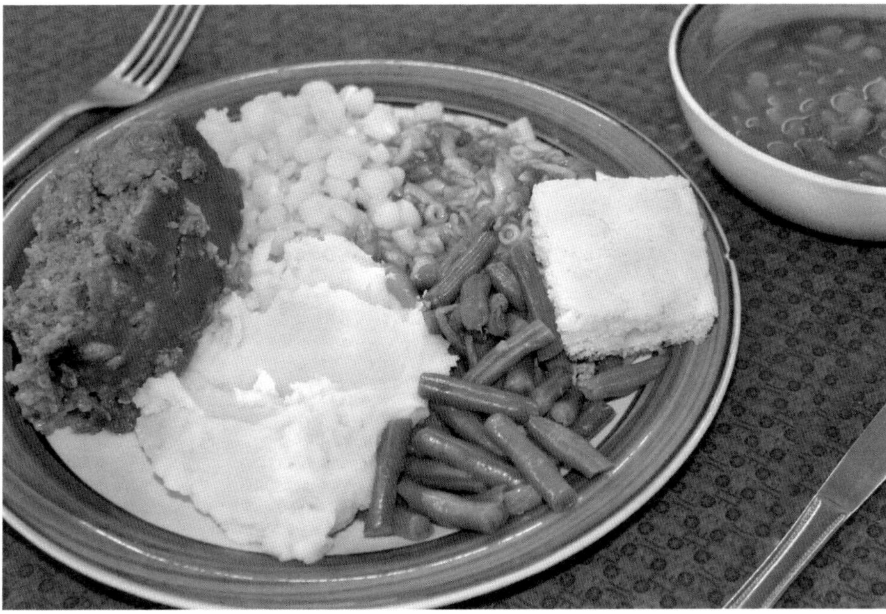

Tuesday's special at the Feed Lot in Caraway features yellow hominy. Hominy comes in both yellow and white, with white being the most common color, but Elise chose yellow for her menu as she already had potatoes and wanted more color on the plate.

corn or the milk stage, as well as in the dried form as ground meal for corn breads, polenta and as grits. Unfortunately, corn is not a very healthy food in its natural form, and its widespread use as a food in the South of modern America contributed to malnutrition in the form of pellagra. Pellagra is caused by a lack of niacin, or vitamin $B_{3,}$ and was almost epidemic in the early twentieth century among sharecroppers and tenant farmers. The native peoples, though, utilized a preparation method called nixtamalization (which is not what they called it, of course) that involved treating the dried corn that made up the bulk of use in that time with an alkaline solution that removed the outer hull from the grain.

Not only did it make the finished product easier to eat and grind, but it also changed the entire chemical structure of the corn kernel. In its nixtamalized form, the niacin that is naturally in the corn but bound up is released, and this renders it available to the person who consumes it. That finished product is what we call hominy, and it was as hominy and not as corn that the Indians consumed the bulk of their maize. It was good for them because they released the nutrients. It was bad for the more recent people because they did not, and for the most part, we still do not. Most corn consumed in the Delta today is eaten as cornbread, which is nothing more than dried corn that has been ground; as fresh corn in the milk stage; or, sadly, as high fructose corn syrup in a processed product. The one time I ran across hominy on a menu at a Delta restaurant was in Caraway at the Feed Lot. I overheard a young customer ask what it was. When he got the answer, he wrinkled up his nose and ordered something else. Unfortunately, that was his loss.

The Three Sisters

Corn has long been regarded by the native peoples of the Americas as "Corn Mother." Some tribes give her a specific name, such as the Cherokees, who call her Selu. There are multiple versions of Corn Mother's story, but for the most part, they involve a woman who provides food in the form of corn to her family by rubbing her body, which the family discovers and are disgusted by. She is usually killed, but before she dies, she gives instructions to someone about how to treat her body, and the corn later grows either from her grave or from the land where her body has been dragged.

The Three Sisters system is a very interesting and complex combination of growing and eating that helped the Indians achieve proper nutrition and a proper balance of life. The sisters—corn, beans and squash—were considered the sustainers of life among the Indians, who believed that the three needed one another to grow and thrive, and they were correct. They grow together, each taking something necessary from the other to thrive. Eaten together, they provide a proper balance of nutrition to support the human body. They were grown together in small mounds called hills. The hill was mounded up about eighteen to twenty-four inches across and anywhere from four to six inches tall. Four corn seeds were planted, one at each of the cardinal directions (north, south, east and west), which has symbolic meaning to the native people. Once the corn has sprouted and reached a height of about six inches, four beans are planted between the corn plants, and the squash are planted around the hills. As the corn grew, it provided a trellis for the beans to grow up. By waiting to plant the beans and giving the corn a head start, it would let the corn stay ahead of the beans, allowing the leaves to spread and the plant to grow properly. If they are planted at the same time, the beans will constrict the corn plant, and it will not produce and may not even survive.

Grown together, they each provide something the other needs. Corn provides a pole for the beans to climb on. The beans fix nitrogen on the roots, which in turn is provided to the corn, which needs nitrogen to produce a good crop. The beans also stabilize the cornstalk, which has a tendency to blow over in storms. The squash grows low, provides predator control and works as a sort of mulch, shading the soil to help retain moisture and keep down weed growth. It has spiny stems and leaves that help keep the critters away.

Once harvested, the three eaten together provide balanced nutrition. Corn is a carbohydrate but lacks two important amino acids, lysine and tryptophan. Both are present in the beans. Squash is an important source of vitamin A, and the seeds, which were roasted and eaten, provide fatty oils. The three were often combined into soups and stews by the Indians or were served together at the same meal. That is way we tend to eat them here, served together at the same meal. The corn is usually in the form of cornbread, served with a big bowl of beans and some nice fried summer squash. Now that is a meal. Yum!

Recipes

Hominy

iron pot
2 ounces of lye or culinary lime
2 gallons boiling water
2 quarts white corn

Dissolve the lye or culinary lime in the boiling water. Drop in the white corn and boil for 30 minutes. Drain and then cover with cold water. Drain again and then run cold water over the corn to remove all traces of the lye. Place in a container and stir until all husks and black eyes are removed. Use rubber gloves. Rinse well and then cover with cold water and boil under tender. Season as desired.

The Mississippians were thought to use burned and crushed mussel shells in place of the modern-day lye because, of course, they had no grocery store at which to buy it. Pioneers often used wood ash, and the Indians could have used that as well. The lye mixture softens the hard husk on the corn and causes the inner kernel to puff up and loosen so it is easy to remove. The hominy can now be eaten as is or ground into a paste, which is what we now know as masa and is what corn tortillas are made from, or the whole kernel can be dried and stored like that until needed. When ready to prepare it, the dried hominy is treated like dried beans or peas and soaked in water to help reconstitute it and then boiled until soft. The dried hominy can also be coarsely ground into what is now known as grits.

Hominy is most often used as a side dish with a meal, but makes a nice breakfast when it is sweetened and served with milk. The product most often seen in stores as grits are quick grits, which means that the germ and hull have been removed, making them easier and faster to cook. True old-fashioned grits take a long time to cook and often must soak overnight like dried beans. The difference in taste is worth the wait and the effort though.

While the Cherokees are not the descendants of the Mississippian tribes who once lived in Arkansas, a group of them did settle there, along the St. Francis River, for a time in the early nineteenth century prior to the removal along the Trail of Tears.

CHEROKEE SUCCOTASH

Shell some corn and skin it with wood ashes/lye. Cook the corn and beans separately, then together. If desired, you may put in pieces of pumpkin. Be sure to put the pumpkin in early enough to get it done before the pot is removed from the fire.

HOMINY CASSEROLE

2 cans of hominy, drained
1 cup grated cheese
1 can mushroom soup, full strength
1½ jalapeno pepper, chopped

Mix all of the ingredients together and pour into a baking dish. Bake at 350°F until bubbling hot, about 30 to 40 minutes. This is an old family recipe from Mrs. Inez Pittman Anderson and the historical recipe section of The Museum Cookbook *of Marked Tree.*

CHAPTER 4

BARBECUE AND OTHER ROADSIDE ATTRACTIONS

According to prevailing wisdom, economic and cultural stasis is good for barbecue, which is, after all, a vestige of the Bronze Age blowing smoke in the present. To eat in a proper barbecue joint is to engage in a time-travel exercise, wherein cookery is reduced to its most elemental, and the past—both good and ill—emerges from the smoky depths each day.

–John T. Edge

If I have said it once...well, again let's just say that Arkansas does not ordinarily come to mind when the word "barbecue" is mentioned. Instead, the mind wanders to Texas with its brisket or to North Carolina with its two kinds of sauce or even to Kentucky with the infamous goat that they cook. No one thinks about Arkansas, which is strange when you realize that all of those people who show up every year for the famous World Championship Barbeque Cooking Contest at Memphis are standing there the whole time looking across the river at Arkansas. As if barbecue can't cross water or something.

Suffice it to say that Arkansas is a barbecue-loving state, with pork usually being the meat of choice. Now, I have to say, and I hope I do not open up a big can of worms here, but I find it interesting that the meat of choice comes from the animal that is the flagship university's mascot. Since tailgating is such a big deal in the South, it is kind of hard to cook the mascot before the game. Therefore, chicken wings are consumed in large numbers by Razorback fans out in the parking lot. It does, however, make it easy for the other SEC schools to have some tasty tailgating in their own parking lots. Come to think of it, Texas is known for beef barbecue and its mascot is the Longhorn. Hmmm.

Since Arkansas is a crossroads state, it is not unusual to run across some beef and some chicken as well, but pork is number one, with the favorite cut of meat in northeast Arkansas being the Boston Butt. Now, in spite of what it sounds like, a Boston Butt is actually a cut from the front of the pig, specifically the upper part of the shoulder, and it usually contains the shoulder blade bone. It gets its name from back in colonial times, when meat was packed in barrels called butts. This specific cut was a specialty in Boston, hence the name. It is a fantastic cut of meat to cook long and slow because it is well marbled—that is a nice way to say that it has lots of fat in the meat. When you smoke it for hours and hours, all of that lovely fat melts into the meat, making it succulent, juicy and delicious. When it is done, the meat is pulled from the bone, piled up on bread of some sort, squirted with some sort of sauce and then topped with a scoop of coleslaw. Yes, I said coleslaw! If you haven't tried it, don't knock it until you do. There is something about that lovely crunch of cabbage, its dressing sweet and tangy, mixed with the tender meat and the zip of the sauce…are you hungry yet?

The good thing about barbecue is that it is usually done outdoors. I say usually because there are some places that have a pit inside, but most of it is done out back in some special barbecue contraption or in a shack following their granddaddy's secret methods and with his secret rub or sauce. I have heard that Craig's Barbeque down in De Valls Bluff used to cook its meat on old bedsprings. I mentioned "granddaddy" because barbecue is one of those few areas of food preparation in the South that is usually the domain of the man. The women can bake the biscuits and cook the greens, but the meat… well, that is a different story. Anyway, the good thing about barbecue is that it is usually done outdoors, which means that one can find barbecue anywhere there is a spot big enough to throw up a folding table and a few chairs. It is possible to find good barbecue in Arkansas just about anywhere being served out of a little camper trailer alongside a backcountry highway or at the end of an off-ramp on Interstates 40 or 55. There will always be pulled pork and ribs, and often chicken will be on the menu as well. If you are lucky and feeling adventurous, there might be some bologna (pronounced like "baloney"). Yes, they smoke it, and yes, it is good.

Roadside barbecue has been a thing in Arkansas since it was a territory. Interestingly enough in this male-dominated industry, its first known purveyor was not only a woman but also a woman of color. Born a slave in what was then Spanish Louisiana, she was named Marie Jeanne but was called Mary John by the Americans in the area. She was sold to a new owner at Arkansas Post in 1806 and spent the rest of her life in the state, where she made her name catering large events at the plantation homes along the Arkansas River. She used the pit method, digging a large hole and burning a lot of wood until it was nothing but coals. Then she placed the meat in the pit among the coals and covered the whole thing to cook slowly. In 1840, she purchased her own freedom for $800, using the proceeds from her barbecues. A short time later, she opened a tavern at Arkansas Post that she operated successfully until her death in 1857.[20] Since Marie Jeanne's days, there have been a number of men who have tried doing what she did. A barbecue business may be the single biggest startup in the state, and it is a sad town that doesn't have its own stand.

While new barbecue stands open all the time, there are a few that have achieved legendary status. Among them is the 2012 James Beard Award winner Jones Bar-B-Q Diner of Marianna, down in Lee County, which technically may not be in northeast Arkansas but it is right on the edge. Close enough that people go down there to eat anyway. Jones Bar-B-Q Diner may be the oldest black-owned restaurant in the South, except that no one can truly pin down the exact date that it opened. All anyone can remember is that it was sometime in the 1910s. Back then, a whole hog was cooked out behind Mr. Walter Jones's house, and the meat was sold off the back porch on Fridays and Saturdays. If a customer wanted sauce, he had to bring his own bottle, which Mr. Jones was kind enough to fill. While waiting for your order to be filled, you could eat skins, ears and tails for free.

Mr. Jones's son, Hubert, later moved the sales side of the business to town, selling the meat from a washtub through a tiny window in a wall that the locals called the Hole in the Wall. He later built a two-story cinderblock shotgun house on a corner lot in Marianna and lived over the store. The third generation of Joneses, Hubert's son, James, runs the business now, although he doesn't live over the business—he only sleeps there on long nights of cooking. He still serves only pork barbecue, although he will cook special orders of meat like deer and coon for the local people. The meat is pulled from the bone and then chopped and served on soft Wonder Bread with some of their secret sauce, which is thin and very vinegary, along with a helping of coleslaw. The crispy skin is still piled in a pan by the window for customers to munch on while they wait for their order.

Another fine barbecue joint is the Atkins City Café in Parkin. It is the business of Milton Atkins, who won that big Memphis barbecue contest several years back, and his lovely wife, Delores. He serves up a delicious pulled pork sandwich on hamburger buns with some of Delores's to-die-for mustard coleslaw on the side. You want it on the side because you can have some of it on your sandwich and the rest just to eat. They have the next generation of barbecue chefs in training with their grandchildren working in the restaurant every day.

Just up the Ridge from Milton and Delores's place in Parkin is another fine barbecue establishment, Johnson's, in Wynne. I had my first Johnson's experience a few years back with a pulled pork sandwich with their signature hot sauce served on a bun with slaw, out of their little barbecue trailer just across the railroad tracks downtown and known as Little Johnson's. The secret to their success is black pepper, which is the primary ingredient used in their rub. Sounds strange, but I can speak from intimate knowledge that it is first-rate barbecue, and their house-made sauce is wonderful. If hot is not your cup of tea, then opt for their regular sauce, which is just as delicious and won't make you sweat. Please note that if you are in Wynne, there are actually three Johnson's locations for barbecue sandwiches. Johnson's Fish House and Diner sits along U.S. Highway 64 and has the more extensive menu, including fish, burgers and plate lunches. It is the sit-down restaurant. "Big Johnson's" is the main barbecue establishment, next to the fish house, and is formally called Johnson's Freeze Inn. Finally, when the weather is nice, Little Johnson's is the little walk-up trailer just off the historic downtown area. It closes down in the hot summer because there is no reason to slow-cook the workers when you can just as easily drive over to Big Johnson's, which has an air conditioner.[21]

Now, if you are a little farther north of Cross County—say, anywhere along Arkansas Highways 14 or 49 in Poinsett County—keep an eye open for Woody's Barbeque in Waldenburg. Waldenburg is a little rice-growing German community that boasts four eating establishments, a Lutheran church and a population of eighty. That should tell you what is important. It is just south of Weiner, which is another little German rice-growing community, though it has a Catholic church instead of Lutheran church. They both have giant rice elevators owned by Adolph Coors, so you can thank Arkansas for your Rocky Mountain beer. Located in a converted recreational vehicle at the intersection of those two highways, right behind the convenience store, Woody's is open only on Wednesday, Thursday and Friday, which causes me much grief if I am traveling to Jonesboro for an Arkansas State football game on Saturday. There are tables out front if the weather is nice; otherwise, you have to eat in your car. Make sure you get

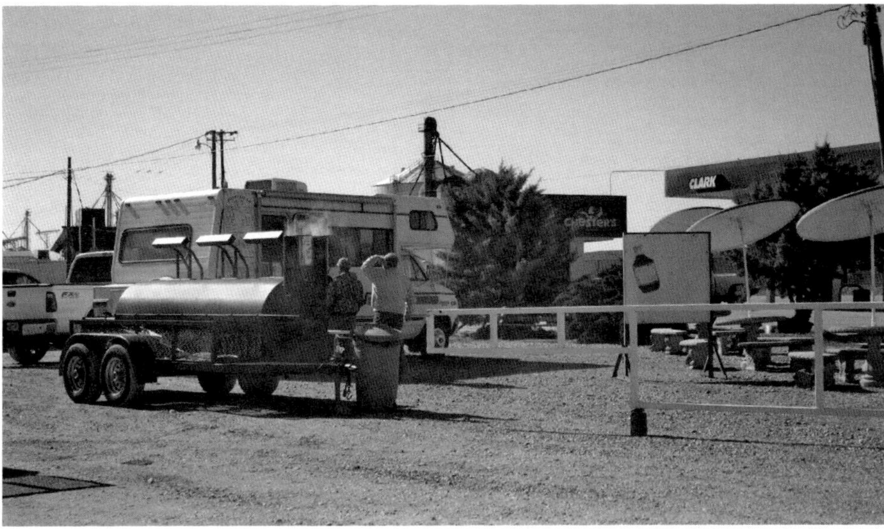

Woody's Barbeque at Waldenburg in Poinsett County.

lots of napkins because it is messy, but it's worth the effort. Woody used to make his own sauce, but it became so popular that he had to get a factory to make enough to use at the corner, sell to the customers and supply to the local retailers that now carry it on the shelves, including Walmart, which in Arkansas is the pinnacle of retailing (as a matter of fact, Sam Walton developed his principals of retailing in the Delta at Newport, where he ran a Ben Franklin store). Woody also sells his signature rub and a nice little cookbook full of recipes that use his products.

Since we brought up coleslaw, which is a part of every barbecue sandwich in Arkansas, let's take a look at that lovely little side dish that has graced every picnic and church social table since statehood. Again, Arkansas is not picky about the ingredients. Anything goes. Most coleslaws in the region are sweet and creamy, with mayonnaise reigning as the primary ingredient. It takes the heat off of the sauce and adds a nice sweetness to the mix. Delores Atkins's slaw is a creamy yellow mustard–based sauce that is slightly sweet and slightly tangy and oh so good. The slaw at Woody's is vinegar based with not even a hint of mayonnaise in it, and it has a kick added by chopped sweet pickles. Make sure you get some to eat separately.

I feel compelled to briefly mention the coleslaw that is really not coleslaw. Several diners report that the slaw served at the Dixie Pig up in Blytheville is actually nothing more than just chopped cabbage without dressing of any

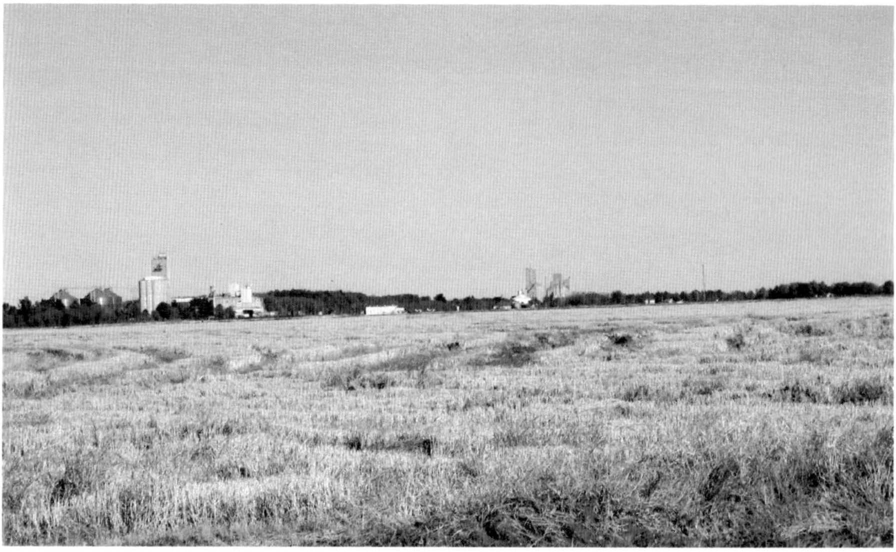

Looking across the rice stubble toward the twin rice elevators at Waldenburg (left) and Weiner (right) in Poinsett County.

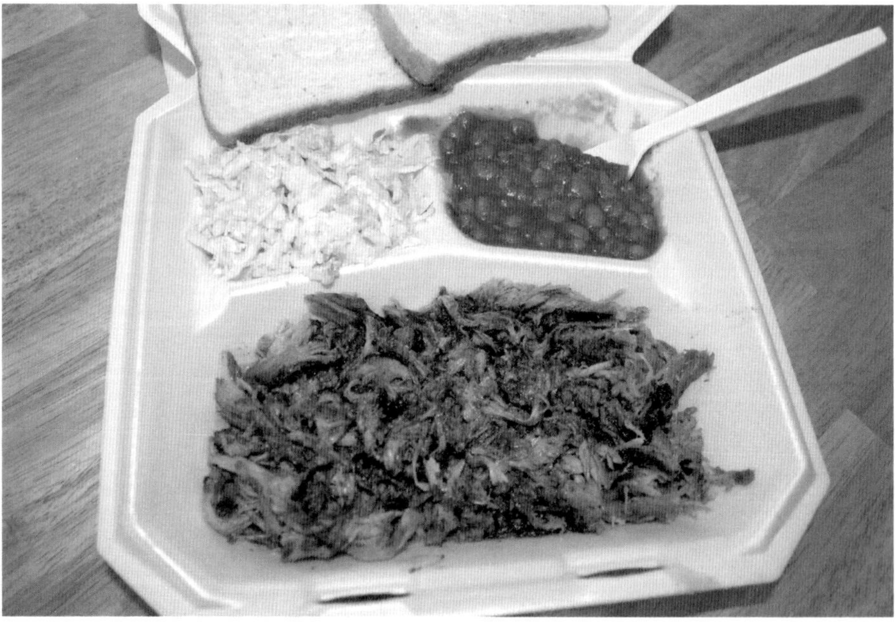

A plate of pulled pork barbeque with coleslaw and baked beans from Woody's Barbeque in Waldenburg.

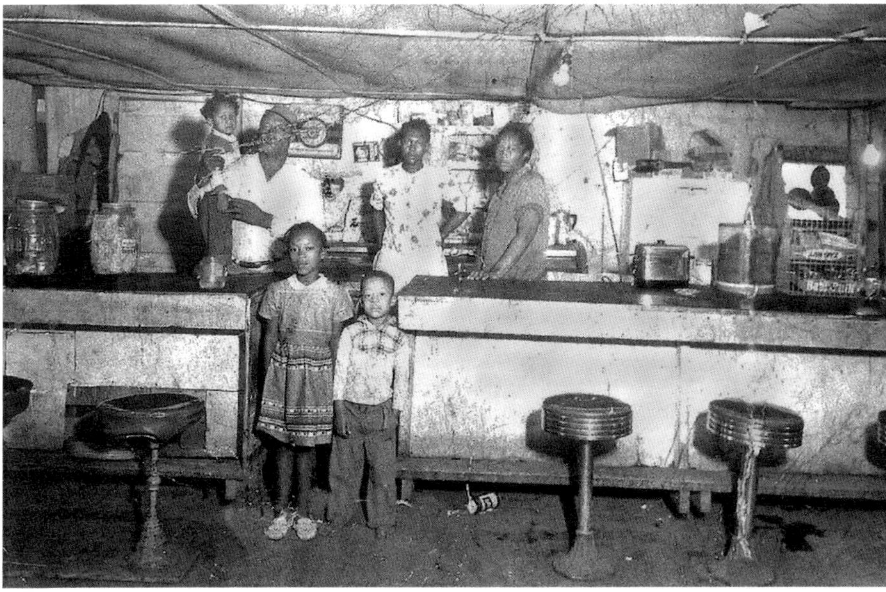

Babe Mason's Place, a famous juke joint in Parkin, Cross County. *From left to right*: Dorothy Mason (niece) and Larry Mason (son). *Rear standing, left to right*: Brenda Mason (daughter), Grover "Babe" Mason (owner), Miss Mutt (wife) and Miss Annie Lou (sister-in-law). *Courtesy Devoria Mason Bolden.*

kind. It serves as a crunchy element but without the sweetness. I admit that when I visited the Dixie Pig, they didn't ask about slaw, and my sandwich came without it. I thought that strange until visiting a local establishment in my hometown in central Arkansas and requested the sauce on the side because they tend to drench the poor sandwich in it, and I prefer my sauce as a condiment and not as the main ingredient. Alas, I realized that they, too, serve the cabbage plain and that their coleslaw, which is served as a side order, is completely different in texture (minced rather than rough chopped). It is tasty though, and from now on, I will ask for no slaw on the sandwich but will just buy a side and add it myself. This may explain why I have never been that fond of their barbecue.

In the roadside eating department, please note that barbecue is not the only item served up in the Delta. Due to the sad downfall of most of the little farm towns in the region, it has become necessary to find alternatives to the regular storefront diner. Far too many of the towns have fallen on such hard times that little remains of the once thriving downtowns, and what is still standing isn't fit to put a business in. Therefore, it is getting more

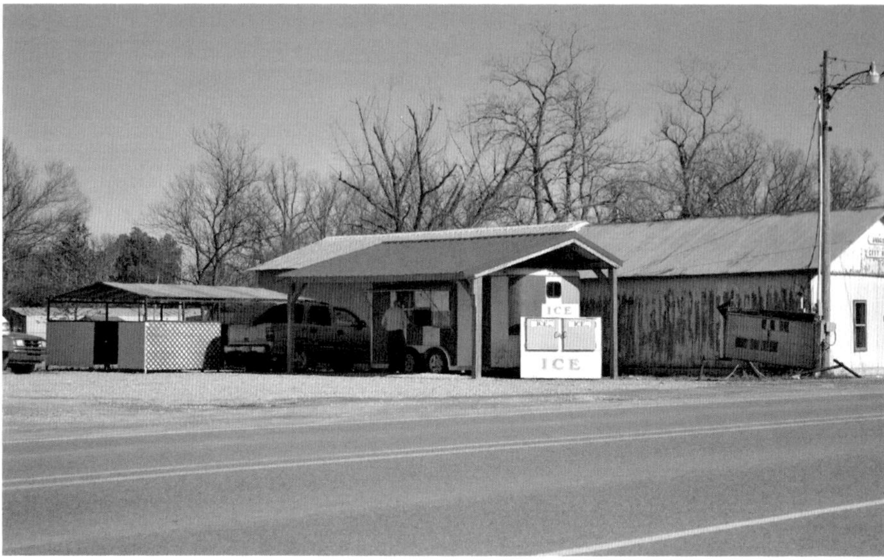

Roadside food truck in Amagon, Jackson County. It has excellent tamales.

and more common to find the eating establishments housed in some sort of trailer sitting in the parking lot of an old building, with a couple of wooden picnic tables out front for your al fresco dining experience—at least during the cooler months, when you can *have* an al fresco dining experience. They are still located in a swamp, even if they have worked really hard to drain most of it. These little places sell everything from burgers to fried catfish, and often you will find another Delta favorite, the hot tamale.

Now, how does the hot tamale end up a Delta staple? The answer is that no one really knows. They were here by the early part of the twentieth century. The people at the Southern Foodways Alliance say that they may have been brought back to the Delta from the Mexican-American War or even that they were always here, a remnant of the Mississippians and their maize-based agriculture. The desire for Mexican food grew in the latter half of the century through a project called the Bracero Program. During World War II, all hands were needed to either fight the war or build the machines that powered it. People both black and white left the Delta by the thousands, and once they realized that there was a life that did not involve following a mule or chopping and picking cotton, they did not come back. The Delta still had cotton, so they had to find another way to get the work done. The solution was a cooperative work project between the United States and Mexican governments. American farmers promised to feed, house and pay

Mexican nationals who would come up and work in the fields. The program was eventually ended, and tractors took over the field work, but the workers had brought their food traditions with them, and the local folks learned to like a lot of it. Because of it, Mexican restaurants are about as common as barbecue trailers these days.

No matter how it is prepared or what it is topped with, it is bound to be tasty, and you will learn to stop every chance you get wherever you can find it until you find your favorite. Happy hunting and eating!

Recipes

As you may have figured out, all of the spice rubs and sauce combinations are family secrets. Therefore, I cannot provide any of them, so you will either have to travel to the individual restaurants and try them yourself or go to the back of the book and see if Woody or somebody else will mail you a bottle. The coleslaw is another thing, although some of those recipes are secret too. Here are a couple to try, one creamy and one with a vinegar base. Additions are optional, and you can be creative. Woody's slaw, as I said, has sweet pickles in it, and Craig's includes apples for sweetness.

German Coleslaw

This one does not include mayonnaise. I have had this one, and it is quite tasty.

1 large head cabbage
2 green bell peppers
1 red bell pepper
4 medium white onions
1⅓ cups apple cider vinegar
⅔ cup water
2½ cups sugar
1½ teaspoons salt
1½ teaspoons mustard seed
1 teaspoon celery seed

Chop the cabbage, peppers and onion in a blender or food processor. You will most likely have to chop several loads, especially if using a blender. Drain in a colander and press out all of the water. Heat the remaining ingredients in a saucepan over low heat. Bring to a boil and then pour over the cabbage mixture. Let it stand in the refrigerator at least 12 hours before serving. It will keep for weeks in the refrigerator in a tightly covered bowl.

Coleslaw

A slightly different version with oil as well as vinegar.

1 large head of cabbage
1 medium green pepper
1 medium sweet onion
1 cup sugar
1 teaspoon salt
1 teaspoon dry mustard
1 teaspoon celery seed
1 cup apple cider vinegar
⅔ cup vegetable oil

Trim, quarter and core the cabbage. Core, seed and mince the pepper. If you would like additional color, you may use half of a green pepper and half of a red pepper. Peel and chop the onion. Cut the cabbage very fine and combine with pepper and onion in a very large bowl. Toss to mix. Combine sugar, salt, mustard and celery seeds in a small saucepan. Add the vinegar and oil and let it come to a boil over moderate heat, stirring until sugar dissolves. Pour over cabbage mixture and toss well to mix. Cool to room temperature. Cover and refrigerate until ready to serve.

Arkansas Coleslaw

This one has apples in it and is sort of like the one from Craig's Barbeque in De Valls Bluff.

½ cup mayonnaise
3 tablespoons cider vinegar
3 tablespoons sugar
1 teaspoon celery salt
1 teaspoon black pepper
1 small head of cabbage, cored and cut into 1-inch pieces
1 small onion
1 Red Delicious apple, peeled and cored
2 ribs of celery

Combine the mayonnaise, vinegar, sugar, celery salt and black pepper in a nonreactive mixing bowl and whisk until both sugar and salt dissolve. Finely chop the cabbage, onion, apple and celery in a food processor by pulsing the motor. You want the vegetables chopped, not minced. Add the vegetables to the dressing and toss to coat. Season to taste. Let the slaw stand at room temperature at least 10 minutes before serving. It can be stored covered in the refrigerator for several days.

Singing About Coleslaw

Big band leader Louis Jordan, a native of the Arkansas Delta town of Brinkley in Monroe County, made famous this 1949 hit song titled "Cole Slaw." The song was written by pianist, arranger and songwriter Jesse Stone, who while not from Arkansas must have traveled through at least once.

"Cole Slaw"

Down in Arkansas
They serve you coleslaw
Chopped up finer than a bale of straw

When you crunch and gnaw
A bunch of coleslaw
Keep chew-chewin' like a cross cut saw

Exercise you jaw
By eatin' coleslaw
Best ol' goodness that you ever saw

You can break no law
By wantin' coleslaw
It ain't nothin' but some cabbage raw

It can't be beat
Just the simplest of a treat
Its fine with meat
Or with anything you eat
Your chops flip flop
You'll enjoy every drop
Your teeth go bop
You'll never stop

Yes in Arkansas
They serve you coleslaw
That's good strategy without a flaw

It's a cinch to draw
A plate of coleslaw
It ain't nothin' but some cabbage raw

Yes in Arkansas
They serve you coleslaw
That's good strategy without a flaw

It's a cinch to draw
A plate of coleslaw
It ain't nothin' but some cabbage raw

No bread
No meat
No potatoes and nothin' as sweet

All I want
Is a lot of coleslaw

CHAPTER 5

BEANS, GREENS AND 'MATERS

The breakfast at seven, the dinner at noon, and the supper at six consisted of pretty much the same kind of dishes, except that there was good coffee at the first meal, and plenty of good milk for the last. The rest mainly consisted of boiled, or fried, pork and beans, and corn scones. The pork had an excess of fat over lean, and was followed by a plate full of mush and molasses. I was never very particular as to my diet, but as day after day followed, the want of variety caused it to pall on the pallet.
–The Autobiography of Sir Henry Morton Stanley *(1860)*

In spite of all the talk about barbecue, the real starring dish on any Delta table is the vegetables. Vegetable plates are often found on menus in the South, with the customer allowed to select from a list of at least a dozen or so different items. Please note for further reference that when traveling in the region, macaroni and cheese is a vegetable in the Delta and, apparently, throughout the entire South. Do not argue about it; just accept it and go on. Occasionally, you may run into macaroni and tomatoes, which comes closer to being a vegetable and will be listed as such. Also on the list will usually be some variety of greens (turnip, collards, mustard or maybe a combination), corn, beans in various forms (green beans, butter beans and a soup bean), potatoes in various forms (mashed, baked, fried, hashed browns and so on), sweet potatoes (usually candied but sometimes baked) and cabbage that has been either boiled or fried.

Salad is not a form of vegetable in the region. The closest thing to real salad you will find is coleslaw, but most likely it will be potato salad, macaroni salad or maybe deviled eggs. In some parts of the Delta, they go for things like tomato aspics and other congealed salads, but I have yet to see one in northeast Arkansas. Raw vegetables, like tomatoes, cucumbers and onions, are usually served sliced and without dressing. Sometimes you may see onions and cucumbers sliced together and served with a vinegar and sugar mixture, but that is about as close to a salad as you are going to get in a real Delta kitchen. I have been told by folklorists that a plate of vegetables served in this manner is called "garden sass" in the Ozark Mountains of Arkansas,[22] but I have never heard the term in the Delta. Here, it is just a plate of 'maters and onions.

Vegetables were often cooked to death in a pot with a piece of seasoning meat over a low and slow heat source for hours. It can be regarded as a sort of primitive crockpot. The convenience of this lay in the need for all available hands in the cotton fields to either chop or pick cotton and would also keep the cook out of the hot kitchen in the middle of the day. Food was needed to keep up strength for the rest of the day's work, so a pan of cornbread was baked early, and the big pot of beans, greens, cabbage or peas was put on the back of the stove to cook along slowly over a banked fire. Dinner would be ready at noon, and then the leftovers were placed back on the stove to keep warm for the evening meal, which took place sometime after dark, when they were too tired to do anything more than eat and go to bed. The cornbread served to soak up the potlikker, or cooking juices, which is where all the vitamins are at, having been cooked out of the vegetable itself. Larger meals were reserved for Sunday, when the family stayed out of the fields and something more substantial could be prepared and enjoyed.

Beans are often a source of contention in the local restaurants because everyone has a favorite way of cooking them and a favorite type of bean. Beans cook differently, and by "beans," I am referring to dried beans, not green or snap beans. To get dried beans, the entire plant is allowed to dry in the field, and then the beans are shelled out of the pods. Usually in the Delta, where the sharecroppers were concerned, the beans were not grown, dried and shelled out because all of the land was in cotton, so they were handed out in twenty-five-pound bags instead at the plantation commissary and added to the tab (called the furnish). Brown beans, like pintos, stay firm, and the cooking liquid is thinner. White beans, like navy beans or Great Northerns, break down somewhat into a softer bean, rendering the liquid into a thicker broth. Clara Nell Green said that she has to have one or the other on her menu every day but rotates between the two to keep down a fuss. Each day, just before noon, the phone will start ringing with people

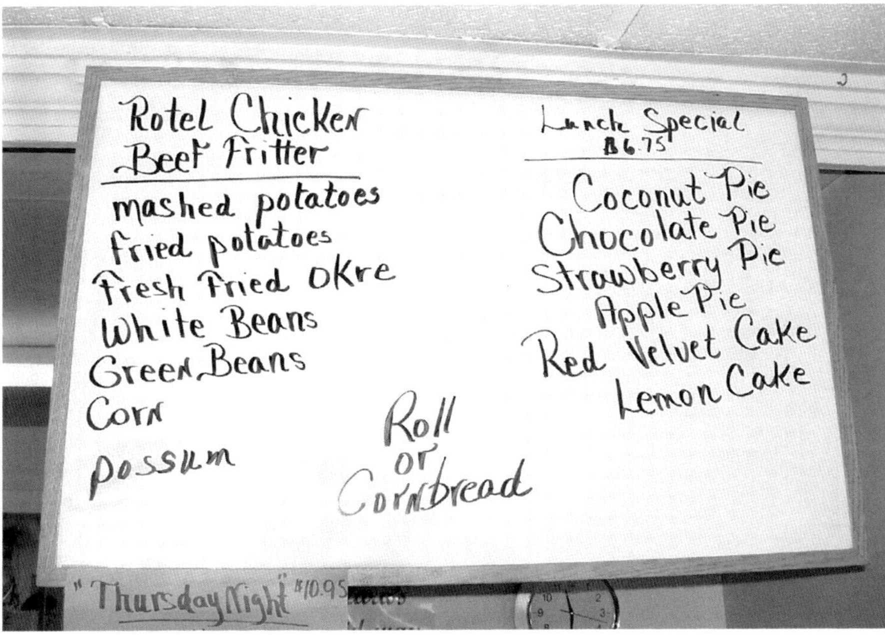

The daily specials board at Clara's Midway Café in Tyronza showing the vegetables offered that day. The listing for possum was just a joke that got quite a reaction from the regular customers that day.

asking which color bean she has that day. If it isn't the right one, they often find somewhere else to eat their dinner. (In the Delta, dinner is served at noon, supper is served in the evening around 6:00 p.m. and lunch is served somewhere else entirely.)

The Furnish

The landowner, or planter, in the Delta worked his tenant farmers and sharecroppers on what was called the furnish system. The planter provided housing for the family, cottonseed and enough food to survive on during the growing season. The food would usually include cornmeal, beans and field peas, salt meat for seasoning and molasses. Some planters would allow the croppers to add other things to their furnish tab, and some would not. The furnish started in the spring, when the ground could be worked, usually around March 15, and continued until the cotton was picked and ginned in the late fall or early winter. At that time, the tab that the croppers had run up during the season would be totaled, and that amount was subtracted from the total amount they were due for the cotton that had been ginned from their crop. The eternal hope of the sharecropper was that they would come out with enough money to get through the winter or at the very least break even. Often they would end up in debt to the planter for the next year, and they would be forced to remain on the same farm again to attempt to get themselves out of debt.

It was a hard way of life and often resulted in cheating or hard feelings. The sharecropper often believed that he had been cheated by the planter, who had added to the bill or not paid enough for the ginned cotton. They would often sneak out in the middle of the night and leave the county searching for a place they thought they would be treated better. Sometimes they had been cheated, with the planter working to keep a good cropper on his land to make him more money, but there were also instances in which the sharecropper really had overspent. The system unfortunately lasted until the middle part of the twentieth century, and there are many Delta residents who vividly remember the furnish system.

Peas are another hot commodity in the Delta. By peas, I mean cowpeas, which are often called field peas, and not the little bright green spheres that most other people call peas. Here, those are English peas, indicating that they are fancy or maybe something that the English would eat for tea. Field peas come in a variety of colors and forms, with the type most commonly known outside the South being the black-eyed pea because canneries wanted to provide a single variety of each vegetable, and for whatever reason, the black-eyed pea won out. They came from Africa along with the slave trade and were often used early on as food only fit for the slaves and the livestock. Whites learned to eat them during the Civil War when they were often the only thing that survived food raids, and they have become an integral part of Delta meals. Faye Hinton Futch told me that her grandmother always grew a field pea in her garden called the White

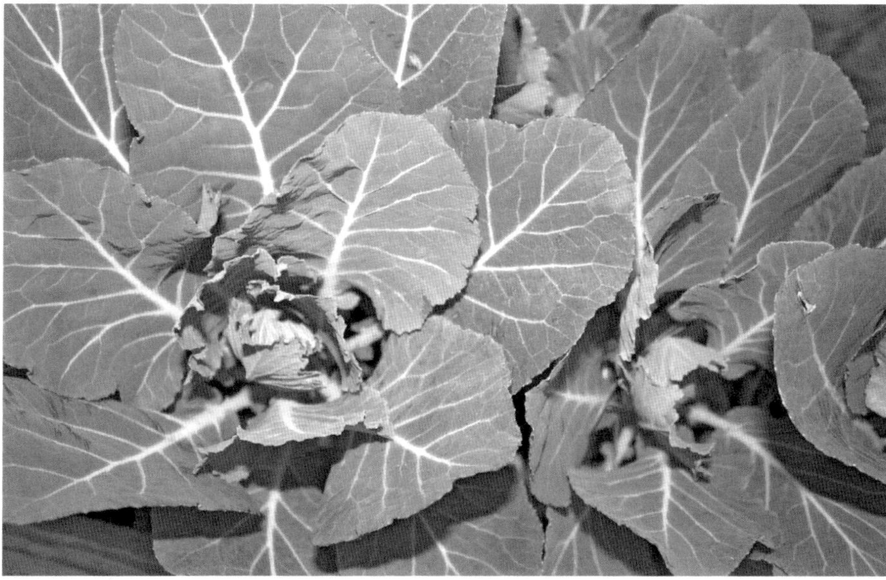

Collard greens in the garden.

Whippoorwill, which is now nearly impossible to find, but it produced a creamy white pea with a dark eye.[23]

Other Delta residents tell me of eating the Blue Goose pea, which has also come close to disappearing with seed suppliers. In northeast Arkansas, the pea of choice today is the purple hull pea, named for its bright purple pod. It often has a purple-colored eye, although there are also pink-eyed purple hulls. They can be dried like beans for winter use but are usually shelled and cooked fresh before the plant has dried. Elise Staggs said that purple hulls and tomatoes mean summer to her, and they apparently do for most everyone else because they are sold by the bushel on the roadsides every year. It was once common for people to pick purple hull peas out of pick-your-own fields (fields in which a farmer would grow a patch for anyone who wanted them). It seems, though, that many Delta folk now are no longer interested in shelling peas, and it is becoming harder to sell them from the field or without shelling them out first.

Greens are another Delta staple coming in a variety of forms, some of which we have discussed already. The most common consumed here are turnip greens, good because you get two crops out of them, the green tops and the bulbous roots, which can be boiled and cubed or mashed. Mustard greens are also a common item. They produce the mustard seed, which can

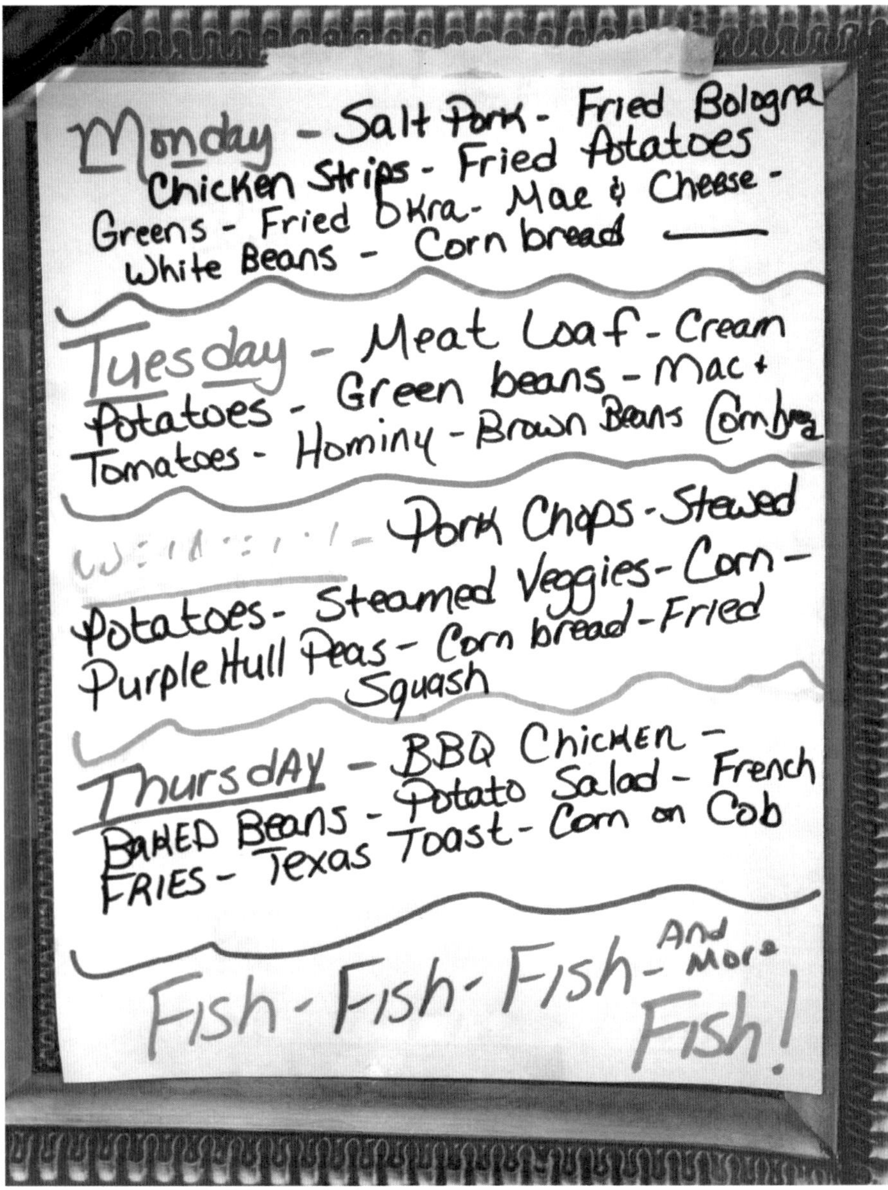

The specials board at the Feed Lot in Caraway.

be turned into the popular condiment for hot dogs, although we usually just eat the greens here. Collard greens are more like kale or cabbage, with a tough chewy leaf that needs to be cooked down to soften it. Greens are usually grown in the fall and winter, and collards are usually better after the first frost, which seems to sweeten the leaves.

Cabbage is also a popular Delta vegetable, usually boiled with seasoning meat but often prepared by a method called frying, where it is not really fried but rather sautéed. We like to fry things in the South, so that it's often called fried even if it isn't. To fry cabbage, start with some bacon in the pan. Fry it (the bacon really does get fried) until it is crispy, then remove it and drain out most of the grease, maybe two tablespoons. It won't look like much, but you will definitely know it is there. Then add some shredded cabbage, cover it and cook until tender. If you like, you can also add some onion to the cabbage. Serve it with the bacon crumbled up in it. It is delicious, I swear.

Moving on to another fried vegetable, fried corn is also well loved here. It isn't really fried either but is more like creamed corn with crispy bits in it. To make it, you need to fry some more bacon and then drain most of it, keeping about two tablespoons of the drippings again. Some people like to add some butter here, which is good, but it will send your doctor into orbit. Take a few ears of corn and cut the kernels off. Then run the back of the knife down the cob and scrape out all of the juice, which is called milk. Add all of this to the hot fat and sauté it until done. It is good to let the corn cook without stirring and then scrape the bottom of the pan with your spatula to get the crispy stuff incorporated into the corn. When it is hot, top it all with the bacon again. How hard is that?

The next vegetable to discuss—and in my mind one of the most important—is okra, often pronounced "*o*-cree." It really is fried, usually after being cut into small pieces, dipped in egg and then dredged in cornmeal. It can also be cut up, mixed with stuff like summer squash and onions and tossed in a pan with some bacon drippings, adding the cornmeal on top. The whole mess is then stirred up and cooked until it is done. Yum! Some people like their okra boiled, but I must warn you that it contains mucilage, which if boiled too long will turn the whole pot into a mess of slimy goo. It is often cooked with canned tomatoes, which is very nice, especially with rice.

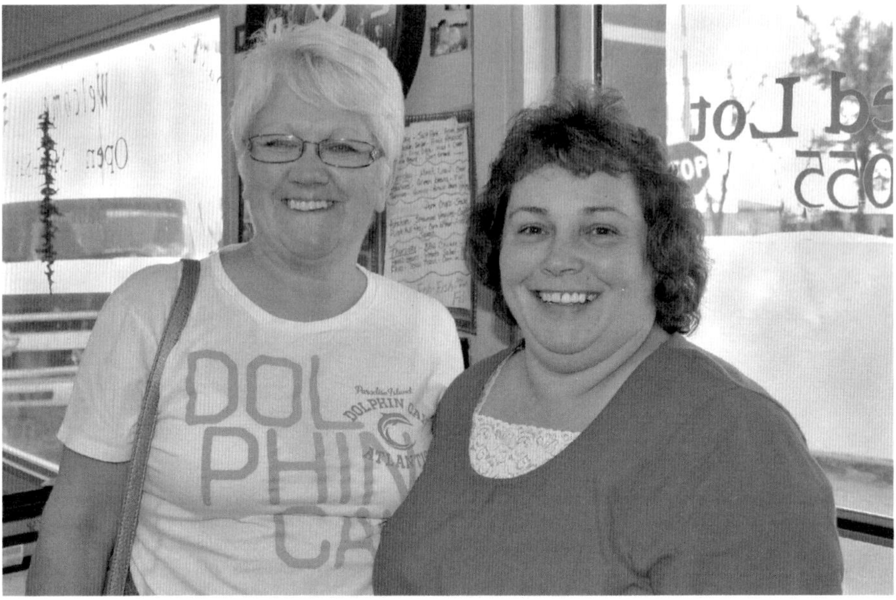

Elise Staggs (left) and her friend and cook, Kim Couch, at the Feed Lot.

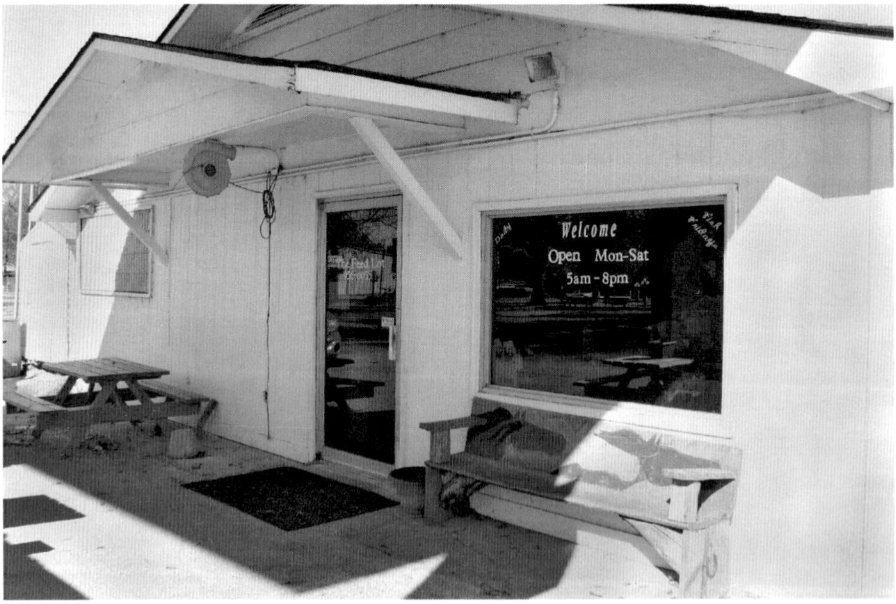

Exterior of the Feed Lot in Caraway, Craighead County.

Elise Staggs and the Feed Lot

Elise was born in Memphis and raised in Hickory Ridge in Cross County, the oldest of five siblings. She moved to Caraway in 1987 and worked in and later owned and operated a grocery store with her late husband. There she had a commercial kitchen, where she cooked and provided meals in the changing Delta town. There were no longer any places to get a meal other than a convenience store or the grocery. She had tables, and it functioned as the town gathering place. After her husband's death, she had a chance to sell the business and did so. The new owners did not continue the cooking, and the town lost its place to gather. Several local people asked her to open a place in Caraway and said that they would help in any way that they could. The town wanted a restaurant, missed her and needed a place that was Caraway Central.

She agreed, and with her new business and life partner, Charlie Faulkner, she opened the Feed Lot in an old convenience store building next door to her former business. The townspeople were true to their word and helped with everything from supplying and spreading gravel in the parking lot to painting the interior walls. The ladies who cook with her are all local residents who care not only about their jobs but also about the community. Since Caraway is a bit off the beaten path and since it lacks things like a community center and a senior citizens center, Elise operates the Feed Lot like a combination restaurant and community center. She has placed a computer in the restaurant and made it available for anyone to come in and use. Senior citizens can come in, eat for one dollar and take home boxes of leftovers for meals later in the day. It is truly the heart of the community.

CHAPTER 6

IRISH POTATOES, SWEET POTATOES AND RICE

Potatoes are a regular item on the menu on the eastern side of Crowley's Ridge and are often referred to as Irish potatoes to differentiate between the white potato and the sweet potato. The western side of the Ridge is the rice region, and rice more often takes the starch slot on plates there. As a matter of fact, rice and gravy is about as common on that side as biscuits and gravy.

Let us first take a look at the potato. The most common method of preparing it in the past was fried. They were peeled and sliced thinly, then tossed in a pan with bacon grease and fried to perfection. There really is nothing better. They are not crisp but softer, more like hash browns without the crunch. Some cooks like to include thinly sliced onions as well, and occasionally some bacon will be added. Salt and pepper to taste, and you have a lovely addition to a bowl of beans and some cornbread. Of course, potato salad is one of the most popular side dishes in the summertime as it is often served cold, and that helps when the temperature and humidity are on the rise.

The sweet potato is a native American plant, although we can probably contribute its popularity to the African American influence on southern food. A member of the morning glory family, domestication occurred either in South or Central America, with remnants of the plant in Peru dating back as far as 750 BC.[24] Plant remains from the Parkin site, believed to be the Mississippian village of Casqui, show the plant in use at least as far back as the fifteenth and sixteenth centuries.[25] De Soto's men mention the plant in their travels as a foodstuff consumed by the Indians, and they would have recognized the plant as Christopher Columbus had brought it back to Spain from his voyage in the late fifteenth century. Although the sweet potato achieved a certain level of popularity in the colonies, planted in Virginia as early as 1648, it was the slave population that may have brought the root to prominence, as it compared in taste and appearance to the African yam, long a staple food source.

Faye Hinton Futch told me that the sweet potato was a food often associated with death in the black community. She said that it was customary in the days when home funerals were common for someone to "sit up" with the body of the deceased, not only out of respect but also out of the need to keep flies and vermin away at night. She said that those who sat up would often roast sweet potatoes in the fire or the stove and eat them during the long night as a way to sustain them and help them keep warm. Whatever its early use, it is a popular item in southern and Delta cooking.

For some reason, winter squash has not been a popular crop in Delta fields, unlike the summer squashes like the yellow crookneck and zucchinis, which are such an important part of the diet. Clara Nell Green said that she has to have squash on the menu all the time, resorting to frozen fried squash during the winter months. That lack of winter squash requires a substitute in that most famous of holiday pies, the pumpkin pie. In the South, it is sweet potato that fills in, resulting in a pie that is smooth, creamy and sweeter than the average pumpkin pie. Delta residents also have a sweet tooth, so the vegetable is a popular dish candied (and is generally referred to incorrectly as candied yams).

Sweet potatoes have been grown in the Delta for years, especially along Crowley's Ridge and in the Buffalo Island area in Craighead County.[26] Members of the Matthews family of Wynne have operated a sweet potato operation for well over one hundred years, with more than one operation in the family. The best known is Matthews Ridgeview Farms, which is Arkansas' largest sweet potato farm with more than three thousand acres in production. During the harvest, it is common to see pickup truck loads of Matthews sweet potatoes rolling down Delta highways bound for roadside stands and farmers markets, but that is not the limit of the farm distribution. Matthews Ridgeview Farms is a certified GlobalGAP producer. GlobalGAP is a private sector organization that works to set voluntary standards of certification for growers around the world. "GAP" stands for "Good Agricultural Practices" and ensures safe agricultural practices and processing standards to assure consumers around the world. Because of the certification, its Arkansas sweet potatoes are consumed around the world.

Rice usually brings to mind Asia rather than Arkansas, but the Natural State is the nation's largest producer of rice, with Poinsett County leading the way as top grower in the state. The cultivation of rice in the Delta, which began around 1900 in Lonoke County and gradually spread into the western lowlands, created an entirely different civilization within a few miles of the Delta cotton plantations on the east side of Crowley's Ridge. Thanks to a system of drainage and ditching that helped to control the Delta's water problems, crops like rice could be grown effectively. Rice was grown very early in the South, thanks in part to the African slaves who have now been credited with bringing the grain to America, but the best rice regions were located along the coastal lowlands in South Carolina and Georgia. The planters who settled in eastern Arkansas tended to be from Mississippi, Alabama and Tennessee and were focused primarily on cotton. Since these same planters were slow to adopt new technology and ideas, they tended to stay with the crops with which they were most comfortable.

Rice attracted a new breed of settlers to the Delta region: the midwesterner and the immigrant groups that most often settled in that region. Towns like Weiner and Waldenburg in Poinsett County were founded by German immigrants who moved to the region from places like Iowa and Illinois. There farms tended to be smaller operations that the families managed themselves, and the differences in farming styles often created rifts in county politics along the Ridge counties. Places like St. Francis, Cross, Craighead, Poinsett and Greene Counties were split down the middle by the Ridge, with the courthouse faction up on the high ground and usually supported by the rice farmers in the west. Together, they would align against the planter elite over in the east, which probably contributed to the fact that Arkansas was always a little slow to adapt to new ideas and technology. When the locals cannot get along, it tends to slow down everyone.[27]

Today, rice growing dominates the western lowlands, with Riceland Foods and Producers Rice dominating the commercial market in the region. Large rice elevators tower over towns in the area and remind everyone where the money comes from. Rice is a beautiful crop, especially in the late summer when the plants—sown like grass rather than planted in rows like cotton—wave in the Delta wind. A small patch of rice provides a great deal of food and a great deal of income as well. Weiner sponsors an annual Rice Festival every fall during the harvest that features a rice cookoff. The website features a number of winning recipes. Smaller producers have begun playing a role in the region, with specialty producers like Hogue

Farms at Weiner, growers of organic Southern Brown Rice, and Specialty Rice Inc. at Brinkley, which grows its Della Rice.

Rice often gets a bad rap for being difficult to prepare and taking a long time to cook. This has resulted in entire generations being raised on quick-cooking rice, which is not only bland but also lacks a lot of the natural nutritional value. Rice is not hard to cook, requiring only a pan with a lid, some water, a pinch of salt and bit of butter. The water is brought to a boil, and the rice is cooked covered until the water is almost completely cooked away. Then the pot is removed from the heat, and the rest of the liquid is allowed to steam for five minutes or so. Yes, the preparation time goes from five minutes to maybe fifteen, but the results are worth it, especially if using one of the fragrant varieties like jasmine or basmati. Give it a try. You will be glad that you did.

Recipes

Old-Fashioned Potato Salad

2 to 3 pounds potatoes, cooked, peeled and cubed
½ cup sliced green onions
⅔ cup celery, thinly sliced
4 hard cooked eggs, chopped
1 teaspoon salt
1 teaspoon celery seed
¼ teaspoon pepper
1 cup mayonnaise
1 tablespoon prepared mustard
½ cup sweet pickle relish
slices of pickle and hard-cooked eggs

Combine potatoes, onion, celery, eggs, salt, celery seed and pepper in a large bowl. Blend mayonnaise, mustard and pickle relish. Gently stir into potato mixture. Chill thoroughly before serving. Garnish with slices of hard-cooked eggs and pickles.

SWEET POTATO CASSEROLE

6½ cups cooked and mashed sweet potatoes
1½ cups brown sugar
3 eggs
¼ teaspoon ginger
¼ teaspoon allspice
½ teaspoon cinnamon
½ teaspoon nutmeg
½ teaspoon vanilla
1½ cups evaporated milk
1 stick butter, melted
1 package miniature marshmallows

Mix all ingredients except for marshmallows. Top mixture with marshmallows and bake at 400°F for 30 to 40 minutes.

CANDIED YAMS

1 pound sweet potatoes
1 20-ounce can crushed pineapple, drained
¾ cup maple syrup
¾ cup brown sugar
2 tablespoons unsalted butter, cut into ½-inch pieces
1 tablespoon vanilla extract
pinch of grated nutmeg
pinch of ground cinnamon

Peel the potatoes. Cook in a large pot of boiling water until tender. Preheat the oven to 350°F. Cut the potatoes in half and place them in a 1½-quart baking dish. Add the pineapple, maple syrup, brown sugar, butter and vanilla. Sprinkle the top with the nutmeg and cinnamon. Bake for about 30 minutes until heated through.

I hesitate to include rice recipes because it is wonderful just like it is, but since they are common, here are a couple of old ones.

Rice Cakes

leftover white rice
1 egg, beaten
½ to 1 teaspoon salt

Drop by teaspoonful onto greased skillet or ungreased griddle and brown. Turn and brown on the other side. Serve with syrup or jelly for breakfast.

Glorified Rice

3 cups cooked rice
1 cup chopped apple
⅓ cup sugar
½ teaspoon salt
2 cups whipping cream, whipped (or 4 cups frozen whipped topping, thawed)
1 teaspoon vanilla
½ teaspoon almond extract
1 20-ounce can crushed pineapple, drained
1 7-ounce jar maraschino cherries, drained
1 cup nuts (pecans), chopped (optional)

In a large bowl, combine all ingredients; mix well. Cover and refrigerate until ready to serve.

CHAPTER 7
GRAVY

Sunday lunch was always fried chicken, biscuits, and gravy, and though the women cooked as fast as they could, it still took an hour to prepare.
—*John Grisham,* A Painted House

I already said that this whole project came about because of gravy. Chocolate gravy to be exact, served on a fluffy biscuit often called a cathead because its size is approximately the same as the head of a common housecat. As a matter of fact, I actually envisioned an entire book dedicated to gravy and other saucy-type food items that are common here, but that has sort of blown up into all Delta foods. This has left me in a bit of a bind because I can talk all day about gravy, but if I do that, then this chapter will be ten times the size of the others. So, I will only briefly address gravy and its friends and move on, much to my dismay.

Gravy is the part of the plate that pulls the rest of the items into a cohesive finished product. It is often overlooked, but if you screw it up, the whole thing is ruined. You might as well throw it out and serve the food plain and unadorned because there is no fixing a bad bowl of gravy. Novelist and now cookbook author Janis Owens wrote in her fun and very interesting cookbook *The Cracker Kitchen* that it is a natural part of life to mess up while cooking and that it is acceptable to give it to the dogs and tell the rest of the family that you "Rernt the gravy." Please note that the term "cracker" is not one used commonly in the Delta. Owens is from Florida, where to be a cracker is a term of endearment, much like "swamp angel" used to be in the

Delta. Her husband, Wendell, however, is a native of Trumann in Poinsett County, so she knows and loves his people too.[28]

Gravy is nothing more than thickened meat juices or fat, usually created by incorporating some flour into the hot liquid and stirring like crazy until it reaches the desired color and consistency. And what is the desired color and consistency, you ask? Well, it depends on your own personal taste. Some people like their gravy thin, and others like it thick. Some like it dark, and some like it light. It needs to be made to order, and everybody makes it their own way. Now, what we usually mean when we refer to gravy in the Delta is that lovely white sauce that is served over biscuits for breakfast. It goes by a variety of names: milk gravy, flour gravy, cream gravy, sausage gravy, sawmill gravy and so on. No matter what you call it, it is basically the same thing.

The French have their béchamel sauce, which is a mother sauce, so called because it is the base for many of their other sauces that have things like cheese stirred in. Béchamel sauce is made by melting butter, stirring in a little flour to make a roux and then cooking it until the flour is cooked. A roux is a thick paste consisting of a fat and usually flour. Milk is then added, and it is stirred to make the béchamel sauce—just like gravy! Danette Portis Watkins Lawrie told me about taking a class in French cooking down at Memphis a few years ago, and she was so excited to learn how to make béchamel until she realized that she had been making it for years. Long ago, Delta cooks didn't have butter most of the time, so they used the fat they had. First it was bear, and now it is pork. Fat is fat, and gravy is Delta béchamel. The difference in color and texture comes from the roux—the darker the roux, the darker the gravy and the richer the taste. Texture comes more from how much liquid gets added and whether or not you leave the little pieces of cooked meat in the pan. Some people even crumble sausage up and put it into the gravy after it is finished. The choice is yours.

The nice thing about gravy is that it not only provides the glue to pull the meal together, but it also adds to the heartiness of the food. This is why it is such an important part of Delta cooking and the cooking of poorer folks in general. It is not only warm and satisfying to the palate, but it also extends the food and fills hungry bellies. This is also why there is such a variety of gravies in this area, to fill hungry bellies in hard times. Those who live off the land often survive on what they grow, kill and gather from the wild. It can be consumed at the time or preserved in some manner and eaten later on. This is called "making do" and requires a good deal of creativity on the part of the cook. Chocolate gravy comes from this tradition of making do.

It is made from the ingredients that most home cooks kept in the pantry: flour, fat, milk or water and cocoa. It could function as a breakfast dish or a dessert, and it was cheap, easy to make and tasty.

Tom Williams of Marked Tree tells of making many things into gravy, one of which is canned tomatoes. The tomato is a favorite food in the South, eaten fresh in the summer, usually sliced on a plate with other vegetables. Green salads did not come into favor in this region until after the Second World War, when all ladies started reading women's magazines and learning that a wedge of iceberg with a drizzle of ranch dressing was the proper way to entertain and serve their families. Before that, fresh vegetables were simply sliced on a plate and served without a dressing other than maybe a little salt and pepper. They are good that way, and it would not hurt any of us to go back to that way of doing things. Tomatoes are easy to preserve by canning because they contain enough acid that they can be canned without the use of a pressure cooker, which was expensive and hard to come by and also a little scary back in the old days. My grandmother had a big old pressure cooker back when I was little, and when she had the thing going on the stove in the kitchen, she would not let us near the place, afraid it would explode and scald us to death. There was no way on the older ones to control the pressure except watching the fire underneath, so they could wind up and get out of hand pretty quickly. So, as I said, tomatoes were easy to can, and out of hard times, tomato gravy was born.

In the Delta, we have two kinds of tomato gravy. The first is what most of us think of as pasta sauce and is solely created by the descendants of a group of Italian immigrants brought to the Delta in the late 1890s to farm the Sunnyside Plantation in Chicot County down in the southern part of the Arkansas Delta.[29] Many of those families ended up moving to northwest Arkansas later on, and their descendants are still here, making what they call gravy and we call sauce. You can find that kind at Uncle John's down at Crawfordsville, just a few miles outside Memphis. The gravy that Tom is referring to is an actual gravy made by making a roux with some fat and flour and then using a jar of canned tomatoes as the liquid rather than milk or water. It is seasoned with salt and pepper and served over biscuits, bread or even cornbread. It turns something simple into a meal for a family.

A close cousin of gravy is potlikker, or pot liquor, although I suspect the latter is not as acceptable in Arkansas as there are still a good number of dry counties, and any association with alcohol is generally frowned upon. Potlikker is nothing more than the juice obtained by cooking any vegetable with water. It is usually associated with greens such as collards, turnip

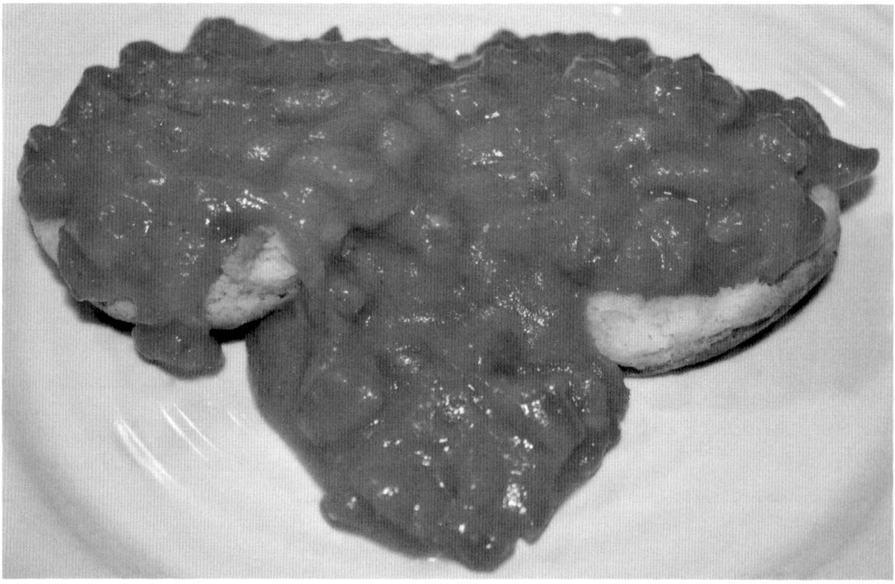

Biscuits with tomato gravy.

greens, mustard greens, spinach, kale or any combination thereof, as greens are often mixed together and cooked. You can make gravy with potlikker as well simply by stirring in some roux and cooking it until thickened. Senator Huey Long of Louisiana, also known as "the Kingfish," once entertained his Senate colleagues with a recipe for fried oysters and potlikker during a fifteen-and-a-half-hour filibuster. He said, "Potlikker is the residue that remains from the commingling, heating and evaporation—anyway, it is in the bottom of the pot." Whatever it is, it is good tasting and good for you because that is where all the vitamins and the nutrition are. Like anything good for you that gets cooked to death in water, all the good stuff washes away and is left floating in the water. By drinking or eating the potlikker, usually with cornbread, you get all of the good stuff that you would otherwise lose in the cooking process.

This same Senator Long also engaged in a spirited debate with Julian Harris, the editor of the *Atlanta Constitution*, on the proper way to eat potlikker and cornbread. Apparently, the southern establishment crumbled cornbread into the potlikker, while backwoods folks like Huey Long dunked their cornbread. The resulting debate was more of a sociology lesson in class, race and gender.[30] Dru Duncan told me that her family often served poke sallet, an early spring green that was longed for in the late days of

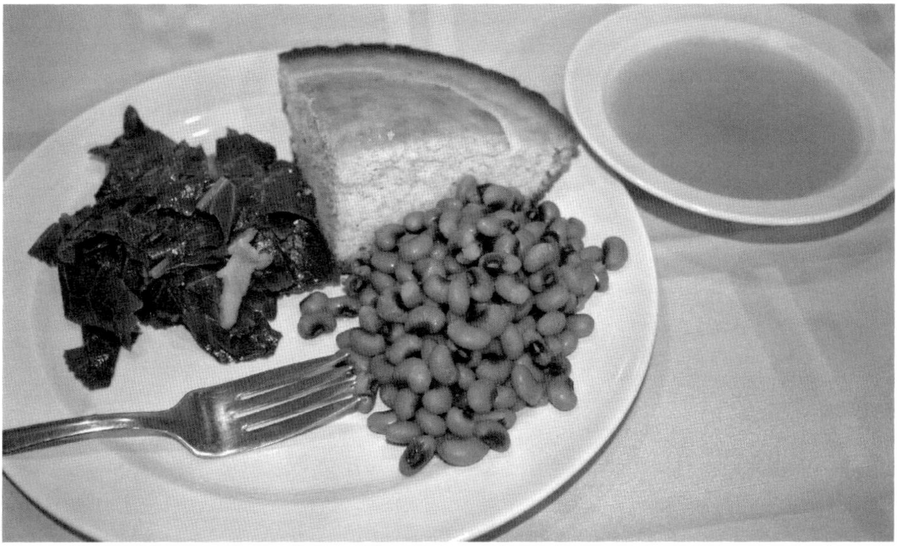

Collard greens with seasoning meat, purple hull peas, cornbread and a bowl of potlikker.

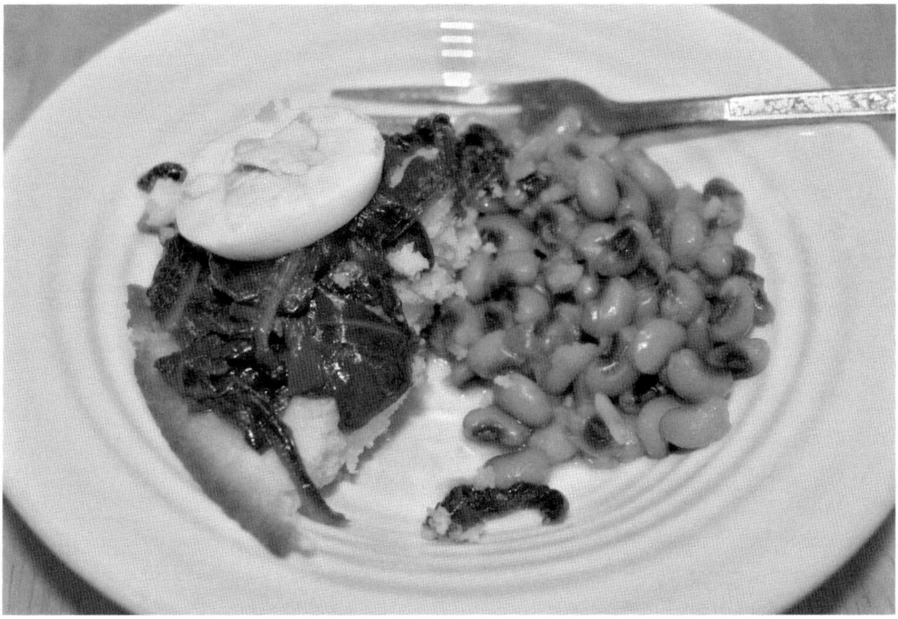

Dru's poke sallet with boiled eggs served over cornbread and some purple hull peas on the side.

winter, by cooking a pan of cornbread, putting the poke sallet on top, slicing a few boiled eggs on top of that and covering the whole mess with the leftover potlikker. I tried it, although with fresh spinach rather than poke sallet because it was winter and I couldn't find any, and it was delicious.

We have only briefly mentioned the receptacle for the gravy, which is almost always the biscuit. The common biscuit in the Delta is the cathead, but biscuits can be of any size and shape. Danette Portis Watkins Lawrie of Lepanto told me that her grandmother, Eula Limbaugh Jordan, would make tiny little biscuits of the size generally reserved for the smaller and tougher beaten biscuit, although hers were light and fluffy. Danette recalled a morning when she and one of her girlfriends, along with her grandparents, downed fifty-two biscuits in a single sitting. Faye Hinton Futch recalled that her grandmother always cut her biscuits with a Pet Milk can that she had sterilized by holding it over the flame on the stove. However you cut them, however big you make them, they will be better with a nice bowl of gravy.

Recipes

These all come from *The Museum Cookbook* at Marked Tree.

Tomato Gravy

1 tablespoon shortening (not oil)
2 tablespoons flour (maybe more; you will know when you are cooking)
1 large glass of water
1 10-ounce can stewed tomatoes
salt and pepper to taste

Melt the shortening in 10½-inch iron skillet. When hot, add the flour (must be thick). Brown the flour until it is dark in color. Mix half the water with the tomatoes and add to the browned flour. Stir while pouring. Then add the remaining water until medium thickness. Add salt and pepper.

Serve over biscuits, alone or with bacon, sausage and eggs. This is great for a breakfast dish on a cold morning and really fills the kids up.

In order to make potlikker, you need to make greens. Following are recipes for both turnip greens and collard greens. Note that turnip greens are more likely to contain grit because you usually harvest not only the greens but the root as well. Collards are usually harvested by breaking off the appropriate-sized leaves, thus leaving the grit behind. Greens of any kind cook way down, so what looks like a lot will cook down to not much. I have read that because of the amount of fresh material it takes to make a good-sized mess, some people will wash their fresh greens in the spin cycle of the washing machine.

Turnip Greens

Turnip greens should be thoroughly washed so as to be free of grit. Remove any objectionable part of the tough stems. For half a peck of turnip greens, use just enough water to cover and ¼ pound of seasoning meat. Bring the meat and water to a boil, add greens and bring to a hard boil. Then lower the heat and cook slowly for 2 hours until tender. Serve hot.

Collard Greens

The blue and white stemmed collard greens are strictly a southern vegetable and are not good until frost and cold has made them brittle and tender. The leaf is dark green and has a large thick stem running through the center about half the length of the leaf. Collard greens are boiled with seasoning meat or a ham hock for a couple of hours. They must be boiled slowly and kept well under water. I usually cut my collards in small pieces because the leaves are so large. Serve collards greens with cornbread.

Poke Sallet with Cornbread

This is Dru Duncan's family recipe, served for generations up in Mississippi County. Parboil a mess of poke and drain. Boil them a second time, drain and then dry in a skillet with bacon drippings. Bake a pan of cornbread and top it with the greens. Slice hardboiled eggs over the top and pour the potlikker over the eggs.

Warning: Pokeweed is a perennial plant that grows in ditches and fencerows in the South. True to its name, it is a weed. It contains a toxin that must be cooked away to make it safe to eat. Most old-timers say that it has to be boiled in fresh water and drained twice to make certain the toxins are gone and then fried in grease before you can eat it. Once it is cooked, it is poke sallet, which is derived from an Old English term that basically means a mess of young greens cooked until tender. Thus, it is pokeweed before it is cooked and poke sallet afterward. Notice I said a "mess" of greens. One never eats a pot of greens but rather a mess of greens. Anyway, if you are afraid of eating a mess of poke sallet greens, and you probably should be if you do not know what you are doing, then just cook up a mess of spinach and use that instead.

Following is a recipe for biscuits that you are going to need to pour all of that gravy over. Many shy away from making biscuits because they are messed up pretty easily by overmixing. Do not get carried away; mix the dough until it is just moistened, and you should get light, flaky biscuits. Aunt Mattie's recipe calls for kneading the dough. I have not tried this one, but Dru said that it is good, and she knows what she is talking about.

Aunt Mattie Bilberry's Biscuits

From Dru Duncan's Great Aunt Mattie

Mix together 2 cups of flour, 5 teaspoons of Calumet baking powder, 1½ teaspoons of salt and 5 tablespoons of shortening. Stir and knead. Roll out, cut and place on a greased baking sheet. Brush the top with shortening or butter. If you are worried about making biscuits, get a mix and follow the directions or buy some frozen ones at the store. You can get away with using those canned ones if you must, but the taste and texture is not the same.

CHAPTER 8
PIE

I sent Lizzie up to help Fannie clean up this morning and I baked 2 green apple pies and took one to her and she sent me some clabber for Mr. Jackson's dinner.
–Nannie Stillwell Jackson, 1896

John T. Edge, culinary historian and director of the Southern Foodways Alliance, "goes out on a limb" in his book *Southern Belly: The Ultimate Food Lover's Guide to the South* and calls Arkansas the "most pie-mad state south of the Mason-Dixon." He may be correct, for residents of the Natural State can talk for hours about a good slab of pie. Pie is on every menu in the Delta, but what really gets everyone excited here is the fried pie. In fact, they love it so much it may have to be the official pie of the Arkansas Delta. Wherever Delta residents find fried pies, they grab them up like they have not eaten in a week. I have even watched them come back to some fried pie chef time after time for some fairly ordinary if not downright awful fried pies—just because it is a fried pie!

I grew up in the hills across the state line in Missouri. Up in the Ozarks, we loved our fruit pies. We could make a pie out of any old fruit we came across, just as long as it was fruit. We are much more tolerant of things like weeds and trees up there, so plants like blackberries, gooseberries and wild strawberries can still be found all over. In the Delta, they are much fonder of cotton, berries be damned. There are some peach orchards left over from the old days, especially along the Ridge, and if you know where to look on the roads around Wynne, you can find some of the old orchards still selling fruit fresh from the tree in the summer. They can make a fine fried pie, but it is not the primary filling for Delta fried pies or any pie in general.

I think the reason for the fruit pie aversion is that the key to good fried fruit pies is dried fruit. Dried fruit makes a much tighter filling than fresh or canned fruit, which is runny. It causes your fried pie to get soggy, break apart in your hand, fall on your shirt and largely make a mess. The Delta has had crop-dusters for years and years that fly over homes, towns and fields spraying the chemicals that keep the cotton fields green and free of weeds. They are now careful to control their spraying and contain it to the fields, but in the old days, they used to love to buzz houses, and it was not uncommon for workers in the fields to get a load of something dropped on them. I have mentioned the strength of the wind in the Delta, so even if they were trying to keep everything where it was supposed to go, it often wafted along with the breeze. I know a woman who told me that she and her brother used to grab a piece of plastic, run out to the field and crawl under it so they could get crop-dusted. Their mama found out about this and put a stop to it, but who knows how much damage had already been done.

Back before the days of food dehydrators, the best way to dry your fruit was to lay it on the hot tin roof of your house or one of the outbuildings, covered in a cheesecloth to keep the critters away, and let it slowly lose its moisture to the summer sun. Cheesecloth, while effective against flies and other natural flying things, is not effective against crop-dusters. Therefore, Delta residents who had fruit usually used canning as the main method of preserving, which means that they do not have good luck with fried fruit pies. Therefore, your average fried pie is not filled with fruit but is instead filled with custard of some sort.

The truly outstanding Delta pies, for my money anyway, are not the fried pies but rather the custard pies that can be found in every café and diner in the area. Custard rules the day over fruit, with the fruit ending up more often in a cobbler, which is like a pie but not quite. Tyronza's Midway Café has a coconut pie that immediately comes to mind, with its extra thick and creamy filling topped with a beautifully browned meringue that is flecked with coconut. Chocolate is always a big favorite as well, although Faye Hinton Futch told me that she had never had one until she operated her restaurant in Parkin a few years back. She said that the black folks are not big chocolate eaters but that she had to learn to make them for the white folks, who love the things. She obviously learned well because there are many who swear that she makes the best one they ever tasted. My personal favorite pie is Delores Atkins's chess pie at Atkins City Café in downtown Parkin, which I have told you is also home to

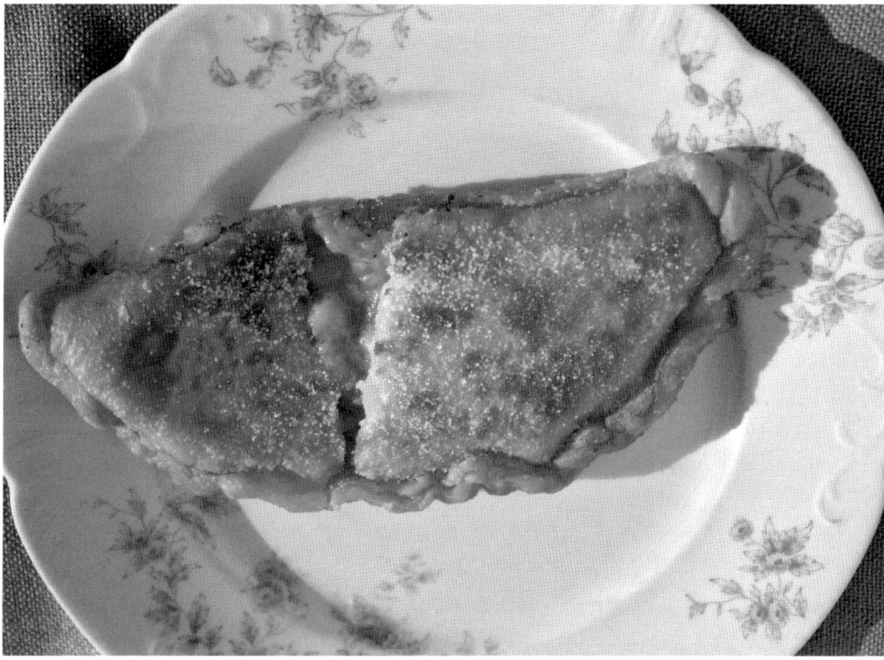

Fried peach pie.

some of her husband Milton's fine barbecue. I don't know what she does, but her chess pie has the most wonderfully sweet, chewy topping over a slightly tart custardy center. Of course, I know that the chewy topping comes from adding cornmeal to the custard, which rises to the top during baking, making a sort of chewy cookie-like top crust. I have made a few of my own, but they never turn out like hers. If you are having a barbecue craving, make sure you save enough room for a piece of that pie or, at the very least, buy a piece to take home with you.

You may have realized that things like chess pie and chocolate pie were possible with the limited ingredients usually kept at all times by ladies long ago. You could usually make a custard pie with the stuff in the pantry, which is probably why these recipes hung on for so long and are so beloved. One truly interesting type of pie was the vinegar pie. Vinegar, with its tart acidity, makes a nice substitute for lemons if you don't have them. Lemons were popular but were often expensive and difficult to come by, so some creative soul substituted vinegar.

Another favorite Delta pie is the icebox pie, which is understandable considering the heat. Making a nice lemon pie filling doesn't take a particularly long time, but when it is ninety-eight degrees outside with 80 percent humidity, no one wants to spend their time standing over a stove. The advent of the icebox and later the refrigerator created a dessert revolution in the South, and it is just as popular today (with central air conditioning) as it was back in grandma's day. They are fast and cool and delicious, and they don't require you to have to cook, roll out a pie crust or beat egg whites to a stiff peak. The crust is crushed cookie or graham crackers, the filling is primarily sweetened condensed milk and the flavoring is tropical (lemon, lime, pineapple and so on). The result is always wonderful on a hot summer day.

Another popular Delta pie is today called the pecan pie but was originally called the Karo nut pie. I was shocked to learn that the pecan pie—which seems like the stuff legends are made from and must have been a grand old recipe concocted by some Delta woman from long ago—is in fact the creation of the Karo corn syrup company. It can be made plain, as in just Karo pie, or with nuts added. It can have walnuts, peanuts, hickory nuts or whatever the baker had in the house, but it seems that one of the best nuts was the sweet pecan, which grows wild here in the Delta. Marked Tree's E. Ritter and Company at one time managed several hundred acres of pecan trees and shipped the nuts across the nation and eventually around the world. Dru Duncan said that the trees were so common in the Delta that she thought they were just poor people's food. Her father would order a large sack of mixed nuts for Christmas each year, and it never contained pecans. Her grandmother thought otherwise and picked them up herself or on halves with the local people, who picked them up off her land for half of the take. Oh, and by the way, it is pronounced "puh-*kahn*," not "*pee*-can." I don't care what Paula Deen says.

Recipes

I could go on for days about pie, but I will defer to another source, the recently published *Arkansas Pie: A Delicious Slice of the Natural State* by Kat Robinson, with some lovely photos by Grav Weldon. They spent a year and a half traveling the entire state, doing nothing but eating pie, taking pictures and writing stories about it. There were days they sampled as many as nine pies! She is a bigger woman than I for doing that and therefore is deemed the pie expert, although if I were to eat that much pie, I would be a much bigger woman too. For those of you who cannot make it to Arkansas to eat pie but would like some anyway, here a few recipes.

Lemon Icebox Pie (with Eggs)

This is from Mrs. A.H. Harrell of Earle in Crittenden County. She contributed it to the fundraising cookbook of the Lepanto United Methodist Church in 1952, which is still a bestseller and has been reprinted more than once. I got the cookbook from Danette Portis Watkins Lawrie, who graciously let me borrow it for a few days. This is the original version made with raw eggs. It is believed that the lemon juice cooks the eggs sufficiently to render them safe to eat. If you are brave, give it a try. If not, there are ones without eggs all over the Internet.

2 egg yolks, beaten slightly
1 can sweetened condensed milk (the recipe calls for Dime Brand)
pinch of salt
½ cup lemon juice
2 small boxes vanilla wafers

Beat egg yolks slightly, then add milk and salt. Add lemon juice slowly, stirring constantly. Crush vanilla wafers, pour into pie pan and pack firmly for crust. Pour filling into crust and refrigerate until firm; freezing is better.

Vinegar Pie

This is from the same cookbook, but the recipe is from Mrs. L.J. Warner. This one includes lemon flavoring, although most of the recipes I have seen do not. If you decide to make it, I would suggest trying it first without the flavoring.

3 eggs, separated
1 cup sugar
3 tablespoons flour
⅓ teaspoon salt
2 cups boiling water
¼ cup vinegar
1 teaspoon lemon flavoring
3 tablespoons sugar

Beat egg yolks until thick. Add sugar, flour and salt. Mix thoroughly. Add boiling water slowly, stirring constantly. Add vinegar. Cook over hot water until thick and smooth. Add flavoring. Pour into a baked pastry shell. Cover with meringue made of egg whites and 3 tablespoons sugar. Bake in a slow oven 20 minutes. (Note: the meringue is optional, and if you leave it off, no baking is required other than to bake the pie shell. Refrigerate and serve cold.)

Author's Note: I regret that I did not get any more pictures of pie. I had usually finished eating it before I ever remembered that I was supposed to take a picture of it.

Clara's Midway Café

During World War II, a good many of the able-bodied workers in the rural Delta were either drafted into the military or away in the cities working in the defense industry. To make up for the shortage, local landowners worked to secure prisoner of war camps throughout the region that would house German or Italian soldiers who could be hired out to work on the farms or in the gins. One of these camps was located in Poinsett County just outside of Marked Tree and contained primarily Austrian soldiers, former members of Erwin Rommel's elite Afrika Korps. These men spent their days chopping and picking cotton and working in some other farm-related occupations. Older residents remember these men marching across Main Street from Emrich's Gin at noon each day to eat a hearty meal at the Midway Café, which was, ironically enough, in a block of stores owned and operated by Jewish merchants.

Originally owned by the Isbell family, the Midway Café continues to serve as the heart of the town. Owner Clara Nell Green offers hearty country fare, the recipes coming from her own family, many of whom work beside her in the business. Clara Nell was born to Alabama sharecroppers who left their home near Waterloo in northwest Alabama when she was two years old to follow friends and family to the rich delta of Arkansas. By the 1940s, much of Alabama's cotton fields had shifted to mechanization, with tractors replacing the sharecroppers. Opportunities were few for the family. Arkansas was one of the last areas of the country to mechanize, and they took up a share

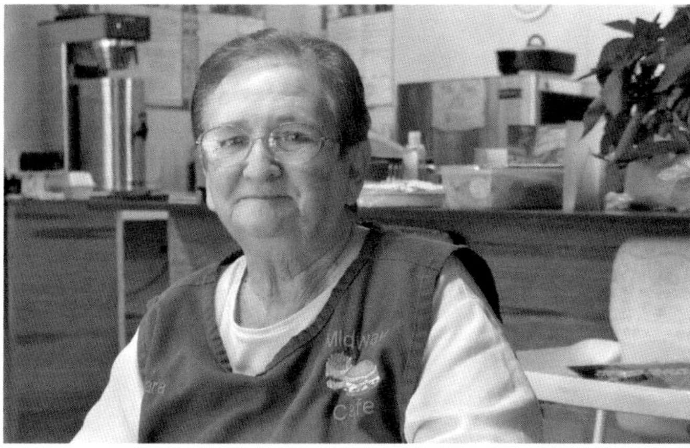

Clara Nell Green, owner and operator of the Midway Café in Tyronza.

crop on land owned by Moreland Barton. The Bartons were good to work for, but Arkansas was also following the mechanization trend; by the late '50s, there were few options left for landless farmers in the region. Her father finally gave up farming and took a job with the local school district as a bus driver.

Clara Nell had married by this time, and with options for farming few, she and her husband left Arkansas and followed other family members to Indiana in 1960. Two years later, they returned to Arkansas, and she found work in a local garment factory in Marked Tree making shirts, a job she held until the doors of the factory closed in 1980. Clara's sister, Robbie, who works now at the Midway, said that she thought the day the factory closed was the worst day in her life. She later realized that it was the best as she was forced into making a change, the factory being little more than sharecropping on a different level. You were still tied to it, the work was hot and the hours were long. Both women said that they often worked through their breaks to obtain their quota and make as much money as possible.

Another of Clara Nell's sisters opened a little drive-in on Main Street in Tyronza in a tiny trailer with a walk-up window.

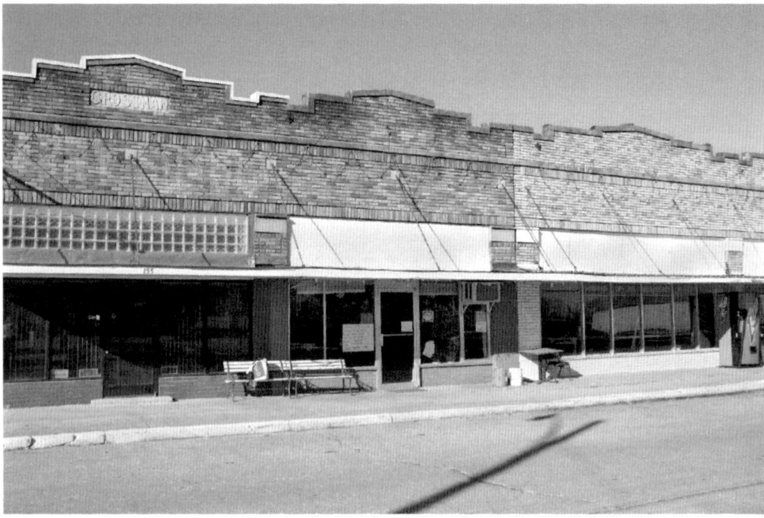

The Midway Café on Main Street in Tyronza.

She later decided to create a regular sit-down restaurant and enclosed the little trailer that held her kitchen inside the larger building, where it remains to this day. Clara Nell went to work for her after the factory closed and realized that this was where her heart was. After twenty years of operation, her sister sold the restaurant to her daughter, who held on to it for only a short time before selling it to Clara Nell. She operated there for many years and then bought the Midway when the opportunity opened up about seven years ago.

The family still works closely to support the business, and Clara Nell said that they each have their own special recipes. She doesn't even know the exact recipe for the café's best-selling item, Robbie's special coconut crème pie. Each day, Robbie measures out the ingredients using her own special set of measurements and her own eye and then cooks the filling. Clara Nell has asked Robbie to provide the exact recipe in case something happens to her, but Robbie said that she measures by eye and does not have any idea exactly how much goes in. She just adds an ingredient until it looks and feels right.

Clara Nell said that the menu is based on the food she grew up eating in the family's sharecropper kitchen. Beans, okra and summer squash are always on the menu in some form for they don't dare leave them off. Cornbread is served daily, rolls being optional, although most of the locals stick with the old standby. They serve as many fresh vegetables as they can, with Robbie's husband, Roland, growing most of them in his backyard garden a few blocks away. Roland sets up on Main Street on hot summer days, next to the old artesian well, and sells his extra produce, especially okra, out of the back of his vehicle. He is also their resident pecan pie maker. He has his own secret recipe, and every Friday, he prepares between twenty and twenty-five pies that are picked up by local residents and taken home for the weekend.

In addition to the regulars who come in for breakfast and lunch most days, the Midway prepares carryout boxes for half a dozen local farmers during the busy times of the year when the tractors are running nonstop. Her menu also features soups, sandwiches and burgers, along with the daily specials and her vegetable plates. The café is open Monday through Wednesday from 5:00 a.m. until 2:00 p.m., and Thursdays and Fridays from 5:00 a.m. until 8:00 p.m. They are closed Saturday and Sunday. Thursday evening's menu features quail dinners, and Friday is catfish day. If you are coming for either of those days, get there early; the lines are long, and when it's gone, it's gone. The Midway's catfish is well known among the Memphis crowd, and there are many who make the thirty-five-mile drive to Tyronza every Friday night.

CHAPTER 9

WILD GAME, FISH AND FOWL

Three slept to a bed on the floor, not only dirt but bed bugs and fleas. Domestic animals, & fowls took possession of various parts of the house. At Breakfast we had Black Coffee, corn bread & Racoon very tough with a little new made stinking butter. We had seen the dogs tip of the cover from the churn and put in their heads and lick out the cream. We did not wait for dinner but left for Osceola.
—Edward Palmer, October 1881

Among the earliest inhabitants of the Delta region of northeast Arkansas were hunters, fishermen and trappers who, along with their families, lived in the wilds of the swamps on little high patches of ground. They survived by selling pelts and serving the meat to the family. Later, though, it was common for these same hunters and fishermen to make their way to one of the local villages or hamlets each day to sell their harvest to either a local merchant or a buyer from one of the larger meatpacking places in the Midwest. It would be purchased for cash, packed in ice in the hold of a small riverboat and moved downriver to Memphis and then on north by train to St. Louis, where it could be shipped nationwide to satisfy the hunger of a growing nation.

Gertrude Marshall Cantrell remembered that her father, William Marshall, brought his young wife from Cincinnati to the place that would soon be Lepanto in Poinsett County in the 1890s to buy wild game and fish to ship back to St. Louis. He later tried his hand at the timber industry, setting up a logging camp along Little River, where he promptly went broke. He decided to move on, but his wife, being from the city, had come to love it here. She and the children stayed and made the rough little town in the swamp their home. Marked Tree merchant and planter E. Ritter was another fish buyer, purchasing from fisherman at his docks on St. Francis River and then putting them in ice-packed train cars for the market. He may have purchased Marshall's contract as he started in the business about the time the other man left the country.

Northeast Arkansas, with its swamps and rough terrain, has long been known as a heaven for hunters and fishermen. During the Great Depression, if it had not have been for rabbits, many people would not have had meat at all. Fishing has always been a popular activity, and duck hunting here may be the best in the nation. Back in the 1950s, Arkansas became a national sensation when Dave Garroway of NBC worked with the Arkansas Game and Fish Commission to spotlight duck hunting in the state. The film they shot at Claypool Reservoir near Weiner in Poinsett County featured more than 300,000 ducks lifting off the lake at one time. Arkansas became known worldwide as the duck hunter's paradise, and it still is. Duck lodges are common in the Delta, and many have their own chefs available to prepare the day's limit.

Fishing is still a hit with the locals, and fried catfish is right up there with barbecue in the realm of popular foods. Catfish Fridays are held at almost every diner and roadside eating establishment in the region. Of course, most of the catfish is farm-raised these days, but that takes place here as well, especially west of the Ridge, where the soil has clay a few feet down and it is easy to keep water in the ponds. Although foreign fish and high feed prices have taken their toll, fish farming is still big in the Delta. The University of Arkansas at Pine Bluff even offers a doctorate in aquaculture. Faye Hinton Futch was determined to make me some of her gar gravy, which is made by frying a garfish, which is a big, long, mean-looking thing with teeth, in a cornmeal breading and then adding onions to the drippings and thickening it with flour. Unfortunately, she could not get her hands on a gar at the time, even though she had every fisherman in Cross County looking for one. Crawfish is another big farm-raised product now, with several crawfish farmers and cookers in business.

Men are usually the preparers of things like barbecue and wild game and fish. I don't know why; I guess they caught it, so they cook it. Tom Williams told of wild game suppers held at Marked Tree every year, attended only by the men and featuring such delights as squirrel, venison and possum. But the most famous wild game supper held in the Delta every year is the Coon

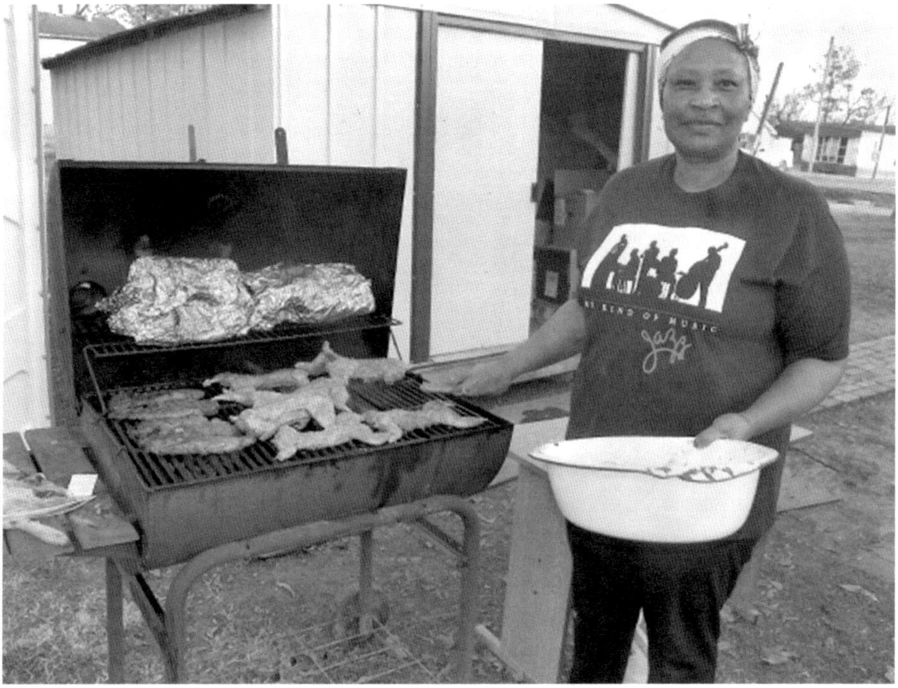

Faye Hinton Futch beside a grill of roast pig, pork ribs and roasted squirrel at Parkin in Cross County. *Courtesy Faye Hinton Futch.*

Supper, held every January down in Gillette in Arkansas County. It began in 1947 as a way to share the bounty of the hunt with friends and neighbors, but the men in the community realized that there needed to be a way to fundraise for various needs and wants in the community, and the Coon Supper was born. The primary recipient of the largesse was the Gillette High School Wolves football team. Every year, the little town of 800 some residents is descended upon by 1,200 souls eager (or at least pretending to be eager) to ingest some of the barbecued raccoon prepared along with sweet potatoes, rice, rolls and cake for dessert.

By 2003, the school had grown too small to support itself and consolidated with nearby DeWitt. By the fall of 2009, the doors were closed for good, but the Coon Supper has remained, primarily because over the years it was a "must" for anyone seeking political office in the state. The money these days goes toward college scholarships for the kids who live in the old school district, and the politicos are still turning out, although former congressman Marion Berry, who represented the First District of Arkansas, began holding a separate event at his house to fill the stomachs of the office seekers who were not as fond of barbecued coon before they went to the real deal.

How the Coon Supper Almost Changed History

As I have said, anyone who wants to get himself or herself elected to a statewide public office in Arkansas has to attend the Gillette Coon Supper, including the man who later served in the highest office in the land, Bill Clinton. One of those trips resulted in an accident that could have changed history if it had turned out differently.

This story comes from another Arkansas politician, onetime governor and later United States senator Dale Bumpers, who is a fine storyteller in his own right. He related in his memoir *The Best Lawyer in a One Lawyer Town* that in 1987 he received a telephone call from then governor Bill Clinton asking if he was going to the Coon Supper that evening. Now, Arkansas is located in a part of the country that is usually warm and steamy most of the year, but we are almost always treated to some nasty winter weather around January, which is always when the Coon Supper is held. That year, it came in the form of a foot of snow on the weekend of the big event. The problem with snow in a place like Arkansas is twofold. First, no real snow removal equipment exists here, and second, it warms up enough during the day that there is melting, which always freezes into an icy mess as soon as the sun begins to set.

Governor Clinton told Senator Bumpers that the county judge in Arkansas County informed him that he had cleared the runway at the airport there so they could fly in for the Coon Supper. Being politically motivated and knowing that if they *could* get there, they had *better* go, the two set off for Central Flying Service in Little Rock. There they boarded a small prop plane for the short hop over to Gillette, much to the dismay of Mrs. Bumpers and Hillary, who were inclined to believe that they had both lost their minds. Things were going well, and the governor, also a fine storyteller, regaled the senator with one of his stories as the plane was landing. The plane hit a patch of ice at the end of the runway and skidded off into a cotton field, where it tipped over nose first into a snow bank. The governor, according to the senator, was so engrossed in his story that he never stopped talking throughout the entire ordeal. The state trooper who was assigned to watch over the governor reached across the both of them and opened the door, and everyone was forced to jump out into the snow from such a height that they all sprained their ankles. The senator said that as they ran away from the wreckage—in the event that the plane decided to explode—the governor was heard to exclaim, "I'll bet we never lose another vote in Gillette."

No one was seriously injured, as Bumpers said, "to the dismay of every budding politician in Arkansas."[31]

RECIPES

SQUIRREL AND DUMPLINGS

3 squirrels, cut in serving-sized pieces
1 cup chicken broth
water
salt and pepper to taste
dumplings (recipe to follow)

Place squirrels in a large pot. Add chicken broth and enough water to barely cover the pieces. Season with salt and pepper. Simmer until meat is tender. Add dumplings. Cover and boil gently for 8 to 10 minutes. Serves 4 to 6.

DUMPLINGS

2 cups all-purpose flour
2 teaspoons baking powder
1 teaspoon salt
1 tablespoon parsley flakes
⅓ cup vegetable shortening
½ cup milk

Combine flour, baking powder, salt and parsley. Cut in shortening. Add milk to make stiff dough. Shape mixture into a ball and roll to a thickness of 1 inch on a lightly floured surface. Cut into 1-inch strips and drop into boiling squirrel stock.

Country Fried Squirrel

1 tablespoon salt
1 teaspoon freshly ground black pepper
1 teaspoon garlic powder
⅛ teaspoon cayenne pepper
2 to 4 squirrels, dressed
all-purpose flour for dredging
cooking oil

Mix together the salt, pepper, garlic powder and cayenne. Season the squirrel with it. Dredge in flour. Add 1 inch of cooking oil to a skillet and bring heat up to 350°F. Cook the squirrel for 5 minutes in the hot oil and then turn, cover and continue cooking until golden brown.

Hoover Hash

This is a Depression-era recipe from the Arkansas Delta. Rabbit, when available, was often added.

3 medium potatoes, chopped
3 large carrots, sliced
1 medium onion, chopped
3 tablespoons shortening
salt and pepper to taste

Cook covered over medium heat until tender. Serves 4. From the American Cancer Society—Arkansas Division's fundraising cookbook, Arkansas Heritage: Recipes Past and Present.

Arkansas Duck and Rice

2 large ducks (preferably St. Francis Floodway ducks)
1 chopped onion
½ cup chopped celery
1 cup chopped green bell pepper
salt and pepper to taste
1 6½-ounce package of fast cooking long grain and wild rice
1 can golden mushroom soup
1 can chopped mushrooms

Cover ducks with water and simmer the first five ingredients in heavy pan until ducks are tender enough to debone. Skim excess fat from broth. Cook in heavy pan. Cook rice in the duck broth instead of water. When the rice is cooked, add the duck meat, mushroom soup and mushrooms into the hot rice. Bake in a buttered casserole dish for 15 minutes. From Billy Scott and The Museum Cookbook *of Marked Tree.*

Red's Barbecued Coon

1 raccoon (8 to 10 pounds)
2 medium onions, chopped
salt and pepper to taste

Wash the coon and cut up. Cover with cold water in Dutch oven. Bring to a boil for 15 minutes. Pour off this water and add fresh water, onions, salt, pepper and pepper pods. Boil 1 to 2 hours or until tender. Remove and dry on paper towels. Dip meat in barbecue sauce and place on hot grill for 45 minutes, basting frequently. Remove from grill and place in shallow pan. Pour sauce over meat and bake at 350 degrees for 1 hour. Serves 10 to 12.

This recipe is from Red Gill, DP (which stands for "Doctor of Porkology") of River City Spice Company in Blytheville. Please note that the directions call for adding pepper pods to the Dutch oven, which are not included in the ingredient list. I do not know what sort of peppers Red is asking for, so use your imagination. If you like your food hot, then add hot peppers. If you prefer your food on the mild side, add something a little calmer. The choice is yours.

Widner-Magers Farm, Dell (Mississippi County)

Dru Duncan spent thirty years working as a costumed interpreter at Colonial Williamsburg in Virginia before deciding to return home a few years ago. She and her husband, John Holt, came back to the family farm at Dell in northeast Mississippi County a few years ago. John was a veteran of Colonial Williamsburg as well and a native of the Smithfield region of Virginia, home of the famous Smithfield hams. Not content to give up their lives as historical interpreters, the two decided to return the farm back to its appearance during the 1930s, when it was the center of life for a number of cotton-growing families and life was slower and considerably different. Things didn't go quite according to plan, and several local buildings that were slated for demolition ended up being moved to the farm as well since Dru couldn't bear to see so much of her history and heritage destroyed. Today, they make their home in the old farm manager's house and have restored several old farm structures that they use to interpret life in the Delta of Arkansas during the Great Depression. Included in the collection is Smith's General Store, which Dru grew up shopping in and which now sits across the driveway from the house, furnished like it was during times gone by.

A food historian and interpreter, Dru said that her research leads her to believe that much of the traditional food eaten in northeast Arkansas is Native American, African or French. The French controlled the Mississippi Valley early on, and their influence is felt not only in the food but also in place names like the L'Anguille and Cache Rivers and Bayou deView. Even the name of the state itself has French origins. Dru grew up on the traditional food, learning to cook from her mother and grandmother. Although her grandmother, Alice Ruddle Magers, owned a copy of the *White House Cook Book*, which is among Dru's many treasures, the women cooked without assistance, the recipes having been committed to memory from years of preparation. Her grandmother was schooled in the art of food preparation by her older half-sister, Emma Ellis Liggett, who raised the younger woman after deaths of her parents. Emma Liggett operated a boardinghouse and dining room at the corner of Second and Jefferson Streets in Dell for many years, and family members reported that there would lines of people into the street in the evenings as they waited to dine there. The train crews from the Jonesboro, Lake City & Eastern Railroad would even time their routes so they would be in Dell at dinner time each evening and could stop and eat one of Aunt Emma's meals. Emma later followed her husband, Will, to Poinsett County, where she operated a boardinghouse on a houseboat on the St. Francis River.

Aunt Emma taught Grandmother Magers how to cook the variety of wild game that often made up the menu during Dru's childhood. Dru said that her dove was "to die for." Among the wild caught foods that graced the family table were fish, frogs and turtles from nearby Pemiscot Bayou or Big Lake. Hush puppies were a usual side for the fish, and Dru said that every family has a different recipe that they guard closely. The fish and game would be accompanied by another wild dish, poke sallet, a native plant also known as pokeweed. Poke sallet contains toxins that must be cooked away to make it safe to eat. Dru said that her family always cooked it twice, draining off the water both times, before frying it with bacon drippings. She said that it was generally served on a slab of cornbread with boiled eggs sliced over the top and the potlikker poured on top of that. Now, if you are not familiar with poke sallet and you just have to try the Magers family recipe, then substitute spinach or another of the milder-flavored greens. It isn't worth the risk to life and limb. I gave it a try, though, and I must say that it was absolutely delicious.

Dru said that meals in her home while growing up always included beans, corn, greens, turnips and the ever popular purple hull peas, which were eaten fresh in season or preserved for winter use. The family first put up the peas by canning but later switched to freezing when proper refrigeration was available, which preserved the fresh taste better. Cornbread was the daily bread in her family, although her grandmother always made a batch of her special biscuits on Sunday. Almost every family had a garden, and at one time, the land that now almost exclusively grows cotton grew vegetables on a commercial basis. Nearby, Blytheville was once home to a Bush's cannery, and Dru said that many families grew a field of some type of vegetable to sell to them. There was a beet farm right outside Dell along the highway. She said you could always tell when they were canning greens at the factory because it would stink up the whole county.

The nearby Pemiscot Bayou was a source of protein due to the fish, frogs and turtles. Wild game was also plentiful at the time. Another meat-centered meal that she says was very common in that area was baked bologna. A whole stick of bologna would be basted with barbecue sauce or mustard, depending on the cook's preference, then baked brown, sliced and served. John said that it wasn't a dish that he had ever heard of back in Virginia but admitted to liking it a great deal.

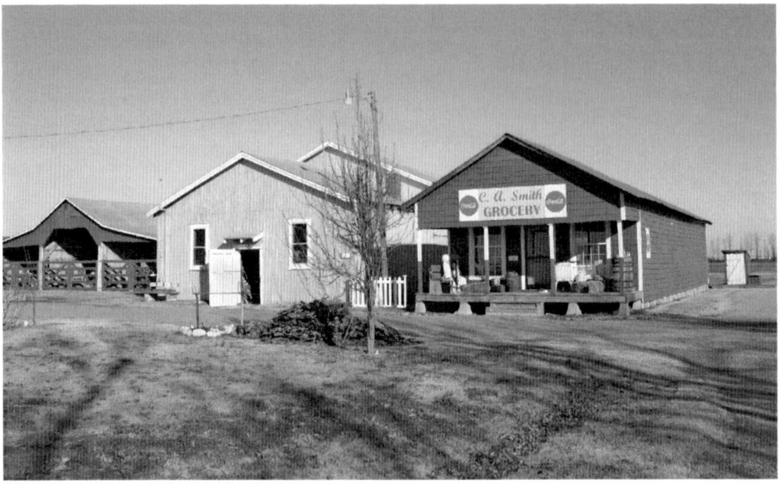

Smith's grocery store building at the Widner-Magers Farm north of Dell in Mississippi County. The store was originally located in the town of Dell but was moved to the farm a few years ago to prevent its demolition.

Dru always had a few food preferences that her mother was not particularly happy about and did not like to indulge. The first was for head cheese, which she loved and would beg her mother to buy for her at the same grocery store that now sits on her lawn. While her mother refused to treat her, Mr. Smith at the store would always get her attention and slip her a slice of it on a cracker. She also loved a concoction called Rex Jelly, which she said was a berry-flavored creation that came in huge jars and cost very little. Mr. Smith would take orders in the mornings from the schoolchildren at both the black and white schools for peanut butter and jelly sandwiches, and he made them from that wonderful Rex Jelly. Dru unfortunately lived in town and had to go home for lunch every day and so was denied her treat, much to her dismay.

CHAPTER 10
PORK

There are a few items that I feel I need to mention that found no other place in other chapters. They both involve pigs, and the real meat (no pun intended) of the pig discussion went on in the chapter of barbecue. However, pork is a big part of the diet in the Delta, so pigs get another chapter all their own.

Because of the heat in the Delta and the lack of preservation methods until the advent of the icebox or the refrigerator, meat was either consumed as soon as it was killed or had to be cured by use of salt, sugar or smoke. Neither beef nor chicken are good these ways, but pork is excellent when preserved in this manner. I also understand that bear can be preserved like pork, and that may account for its heavy use as a food early on. Of course, clearing the land of forests and primarily of cane brakes has reduced the bear population, so we eat pork instead. Cane brakes, for those who are not familiar, are areas with a thick growth of a plant called *Arundinaria gigantea* by the botanists and river cane by the rest of us. It is an American relative of bamboo, and it grows like crazy where there is fertile soil and lots of water, and bears like to hang out in them. Since Delta farmers wanted to grow cotton and not be bothered by bears, they cleared them both out. Arkansas used to have so many bears that its nickname was the Bear State, and bear oil was a primary export. There is even a town on the White River called Oil Trough that is named for the large amount of bear oil that they used to produce there, but I digress. Let's get back to pork.

Hog killings used to be the big event of the year on Delta farms.[32] They were done in the late fall or early winter when the temperatures were cool and the meat would not spoil as easily. Every part of the pig was used. Faye Hinton Futch's grandmother always said that you use everything from the rooter to the tooter. The skin of the pig was where a lot of the fat was located, and that skin would be cut off and placed in large heavy pots over the fire to render out the fat, or lard, for use in cooking the rest of the year.

Lard has gotten a bad rap over the years, fueled by the people who make shortening and vegetable oils, but thanks to the foodies, it is making a comeback. Left over from the rendering process would be bits of skin called cracklings that were crunchy and very tasty, and they were often skimmed off for use in making cornbread. It has a nice crispy crunch and a good pork flavor. My friend Marion Haynes from up at Yarbro in Mississippi County said that every year at hog killing time, his grandfather would scoop a bunch out of the rendering kettle and demand some crackling cornbread be made right then. If you do not finish them all off in your cornbread, they could also be dried out and then deep fried to make the snack we know as pork rinds. Pork rinds are fun little things because when they are fried they puff up and into a nice crunchy snack. They can be salted or covered with other toppings like barbecue spice and are actually fairly healthy for you. They are popular almost everywhere but nowhere as much as in the Delta. I realized this one day while waiting for a pizza in a convenience store in Parkin (the barbecue place was closed already, so I had to do what I had to do). Anyway, I realized that in that single store, in a town of 1,500 residents, there was a sixteen-foot-long section of display space dedicated to nothing but pork rinds in every flavor imaginable. The variety was staggering.

A second product of the hog butchering process that has retained a loyal following among Delta natives are chitterlings, or chit'lins. Chit'lins are the cleaned-out small intestines of the pig that are cooked in a number of ways, including boiling, frying or baking. Because they are intestines, they need to be cleaned very, very thoroughly to ensure that there is no fecal matter left inside. They are then rinsed several times, cut into small pieces about two inches long, cooked with onions, garlic, salt and pepper for a couple of hours and then topped with hot sauce and eaten. At least, this is what I have been told because I do not come from a chit'lin-eating people and have not had any prepared for me by anyone who is. I understand that they do not have a pleasant aroma when cooking. One morning, I saw a bunch of trucks gathered around the old barbecue trailer in Tyronza and asked my boss, Linda, what was going on there as the barbecue restaurant had closed some months before. She told me that Teddy Prestidge was cooking chit'lins for the men down there because their wives wouldn't let them cook them at home. I asked why they could not cook them at home, and she said because they smell bad. I asked how bad, and she said, "They smell like shit cooking." Needless to say, I did not venture down to the barbecue trailer for lunch that day.

For those who love the things and no longer have access to a hog killing, chit'lins are available these days commercially. They come in big red plastic tubs, and some families cook them for the holidays just like Bradley's family cooks chicken and dumplings. You can get regular chit'lins that you have to clean yourself or fancy chit'lins that are already cleaned. I understand that if you have ever gotten one that was not cleaned properly, it is something you will never get over; most self-respecting cooks insist on cleaning their own. Bradley told me that a woman came into the store that he works at and asked for the chit'lins you clean yourself, "not the uppity kind that are already cleaned."

Probably the most popular item from the pig that is used in Delta cooking is bacon grease, or drippings. It is the main frying item around because unlike shortening or vegetable oil, it imparts a nice flavor to the food, much like lard. It used to be common to use lard or bacon grease as a spread for bread in place of butter, which many Delta sharecroppers had little access to. Delta cooks used to all insist on a bacon-greased cast-iron skillet as the only possible receptacle in which to bake a pan of cornbread. It adds a nice touch to beans, greens, fried potatoes and just about any other vegetable that you can think of cooking. The nice thing about bacon grease is that it is easy to come by, just fry a piece of bacon, and you get bacon grease and a nice hot pan in which to proceed. Of course, people who fry a lot keep all of their leftover grease in little cans or jars on the stove because bacon always makes way more grease than needed at the time for flavoring. If you have never tried it, give it try. You will be glad you did.

Cooking with Cotton

Elise Staggs told me that the people up at Caraway will eat just about anything she fixes except rice. There is something about cotton farmers and rice farmers that does not mix very well. She said that if she could find a way to cook cotton, she thinks they would eat that. What she may not realize is that there is a way to cook with cotton, or at least there used to be a way: Crisco!

Crisco is actually a modification of the name "crystalized cottonseed oil," and that was the main ingredient for years. It was not the first shortening product to be made of cottonseed oil—that honor belongs to Cottolene. Cottolene was half cottonseed oil and half beef tallow and was created as the first mass-produced and marketed alternative to lard. Senator Huey P. Long, who made an appearance in these pages earlier, spent some time in his youth as a traveling Cottolene salesman, and it was at a Cottolene bakeoff in Shreveport where he met Rose McConnell, the woman who would become his wife. Even though Huey Long was a senator and governor from our neighbor to the south, Louisiana, he played an important role in the political process in Arkansas when he brought his traveling election show on the road to help elect Hattie Wyatt Caraway of Jonesboro to the United States Senate, but that is another story.

While Cottolene has been gone since about 1950, Crisco is still with us today, although it is made with a combination of soybean and palm oils brought about by the desire to lower trans fat, which apparently contributes to the risk of coronary heart disease. It is also the product that most contributed to the demise of lard as a cooking fat. Maybe they should just eat rice.

Recipes

Cracklin' Cornbread

This is from the Arkansas Dutch Oven Society and can easily be adapted to a cast-iron skillet and an oven.

½ cup oil, or drippings, plus 3 teaspoons
2 cups corn meal
2 cups all-purpose flour
2 to 4 tablespoons sugar

2 tablespoons baking powder
1 teaspoon salt
2 cups milk
2 eggs, beaten
1½ cup cracklings

Preheat a 12-inch Dutch oven to 425°F (this is achieved by placing twenty-one coals on top and ten on the bottom), or heat your oven to 425°F. Heat oil for 3 minutes. Combine dry ingredients and add milk and eggs. Mix until blended. Pour in melted drippings and cracklings. Stir well. Pour into hot Dutch oven or skillet and bake 20 to 25 minutes or until a toothpick inserted in the center comes out clean. If baking in a Dutch oven, during the last 5 to 10 minutes of baking time, you may need to remove the bottom heat to prevent overbrowning.

HAM HOCK WITH CORNMEAL DUMPLINGS

This is one of the historical recipes from *The Museum Cookbook* at Marked Tree and includes not only pork but cut corn as well.

1 good size ham hock, cured or fresh
1 cup flour
2 cups corn meal
salt and pepper to taste
1 onion, chopped
1 to 2 eggs

Boil the ham hock until it is tender. Remove the meat from the broth. Mix together the flour, corn meal, salt, pepper and onion in a mixing bowl and mix well. Stir in the egg and then add enough hot broth to make the dough enough to form into balls. With your hands, form the dough into balls about the size of small eggs. Drop them into the broth and bring the pot back to a boil. Do not stir the pot too often once it begins to boil. Pick the meat from the ham hocks and add into the pot.

FAYE HINTON FUTCH

Faye Hinton Futch is a true child of the Delta. She was born on a Cross County cotton plantation called Burr Place, near Coldwater, shortly after World War II. Burr Place and Birdeye were two separate plantations operated by the Smith brothers, and while Birdeye is still fairly well known, Burr Place has slipped from memory. Years earlier, her grandfather, U.L. Hinton, had been put off Burr Place for organizing workers. He may have been involved in the Southern Tenant Farmers Union that was fairly active in Cross County in the 1930s. It had been formed over in Poinsett County at Tyronza in 1934, and within a couple of years, it had spread to several southern states and boasted a membership nearing forty thousand, both black and white sharecroppers and tenant farmers. U.L.'s maternal grandfather was a white slave owner from Henning, Tennessee.

For the first couple of years of her life, her father wanted out of the sharecropping life and supported Faye and her mother by playing semiprofessional baseball for a man named Julius over in Crittenden County. He owned a large farm southeast of Crawsfordsville, where he had built a baseball field for his Julius Greyhounds to play on. Baseball in those days was more than the national pastime in eastern Arkansas; it was an obsession. Delta businessmen and planters would start teams that early on consisted of the local boys, but as the stakes got higher, they would bring in what they called ringers—good players from other areas to star on their teams. Entire towns would shut down for baseball games back in those days. Faye's father was a very skilled player, and Mr. Julius paid him seventeen dollars a week, plus his uniform and travel expenses to play on his team. The money was good enough that he supported Faye and her mother completely on his baseball wages. Later, as more children began arriving, the baseball became supplemental, and he moved the family to Parkin, where he worked in a variety of jobs, including the Missouri Pacific Railroad, the International Harvester dealer in Parkin and the Parkin ice plant.

The family lived in one of three African American neighborhoods in Parkin, and the neighborhood was also the center of the black business district in Parkin. Parkin Avenue was the center of business activity in the town. It was bisected by Arkansas Route 75, now called the 75 Spur. East of the road was the white business district, and west was the black business district, Dyes Bottoms. Faye grew up in the middle of that district, which was loosely organized with most people operating their businesses out of their homes. At one time, she can remember nine separate juke joints in operation in Dyes Bottoms. Juke joints were the social hub for the black families of Parkin and the farms that surrounded the town for several miles—places like the Cherry Place, Togo, Burr Place, Twist and Birdeye. She remembered crowds of people walking miles into Parkin on Saturday to spend the day shopping, eating, drinking, dancing and enjoying the music coming out of "the Joints."

Her father was one of the few black men to own a car when she was young, and he would drive over to Memphis on weekends and drive some of the blues legends over to Parkin to play. People like B.B. King and Muddy Waters were regulars in joints like Babe Mason's Place, which featured a juke joint downstairs and a brothel upstairs. Faye remembered meeting Muddy Waters at the age of eight when her father brought him to town to play. Howlin' Wolf was born Chester Arthur Burnett and grew up out on the Togo farm just north of Parkin and came back to his old home to play often. Rock legend Carl Perkins came up with his hit song "Blue Suede Shoes" after performing a show in Parkin, where he overheard a man in the crowd tell his date to watch out for his new blue suede shoes.

The juke joints were the social centers of Delta communities like Parkin. They were business opportunities for many folks, women as well as men. They were popular for the night life and were places where black community members ate their meals and socialized during the slow times. Birthday parties were held in them, and card games went on for days there. Baseball games were also a weekend feature, and many of the rural joints had a baseball field next to the building. One of the more popular food items in the joints was the pork chop sandwich, which featured a bone-in pork chop that was seasoned and dredged in flour and then fried to golden perfection and served with lettuce, tomato and mayonnaise on two fluffy pieces of Wonder Bread. Patrons could also get things like hamburgers and fried bologna sandwiches served with a bottle of Coca-Cola or a cold beer.

Faye's maternal grandmother moved in when the babies started coming and stayed on, twelve of them before they were through. Her grandmother took care of the cooking, growing what she could and buying the rest, feeding three adults and twelve children on twenty dollars per week, although she said that they only ate two meals a day back then, breakfast and supper. Prominent among Faye's memories of her grandmother's cooking was her jar of buttermilk that she made every week and kept out on the counter at room temperature. Once a week, she would replenish the supply in the jar by adding enough powdered milk to fill the gallon jar. She made all of her biscuits and cornbread out of this buttermilk, and every morning, when she finished her batch of biscuits, she would pinch off a piece of the dough, throw it in the jar to feed it and stir the mixture every morning. She said it was considered a treat to be given a glass of the buttermilk to drink by her grandmother; it was rich and delicious.

Every morning for breakfast, her grandmother would make twenty biscuits, cutting them in circles with a PET milk can she had cut both ends out of and would sterilize by holding it over the stove burner. The rest of the leftover dough would often be used to make a dessert for the evening meal. One of her favorites was butter rolls, a rich, creamy biscuit-based concoction that was poached in the oven in a sweet milk sauce. Her paternal grandmother, Celester Hinton, devised a butter roll recipe that she called cheese butter rolls that used the commodity cheddar cheese that the family received at that time. This was so popular with her father that her mother and maternal grandmother learned to make it as well. It is still prepared for every family event.

One of those events was the annual hog killing that provided the family with meat for the coming year. It took place in the late fall when the weather was cool enough. Delta families in those days made use of every part of the animal. Among the children's favorite parts of the event was watching their grandmother make head cheese. She would boil the whole head in a large pot, and then when everything was tender and cool enough to touch, she would pull every usable piece of meat off it and put then in a large loaf pan, packing them firmly. She would then pour the stock from the pot over the meat in the pan, cover it and place it in the refrigerator to cool overnight. By morning, the stock had congealed into a gelatinous form like aspic, and the whole affair could be turned out and sliced like a luncheon meat. Faye said that all of the children would watch their grandmother pick off the meat, half horrified at the whole head lying there and half starved thinking about their first taste of that finished head cheese served on a saltine cracker.

The Hinton family is not physically located as close as they once were, but they gather on every occasion one can think of to celebrate and eat. An annual summer event for the family is held in her parents' backyard on Parkin Street, where they prepare a large pot of frogmore stew. Frogmore stew tastes a lot better than it sounds. It is not a stew, and there is not a frog to be found in it. It is, in fact, a traditional Lowcountry boil of Andouille sausage, corn and potatoes and uses local crawfish, called mudbugs, instead of Carolina shrimp. It is cooked outdoors in a large cast-iron pot that sits atop concrete blocks. A fire is built underneath, and the pot, filled with water and Old Bay seasoning, is started boiling. The potatoes are added first and cooked for about fifteen minutes. The corn and sausage are added next and cooked for maybe five more minutes. Finally, the crawfish are dumped in. The whole pot is boiled until the crawfish turn a bright-red color, indicating that they are done. The pot is drained and the contents poured out onto a newspaper-lined table for everyone to grab what they want. At the Hinton house, the cast-iron pot is too heavy to lift, so they scoop everything into large stockpots and take them in the house to finish the draining process. The daylong ritual draws many nonfamily members as well, most of the neighbors being old family friends.

Almost every summer weekend, as well as holidays and birthdays for young and old, will find the family gathered together focused on first one eating event and then another. In

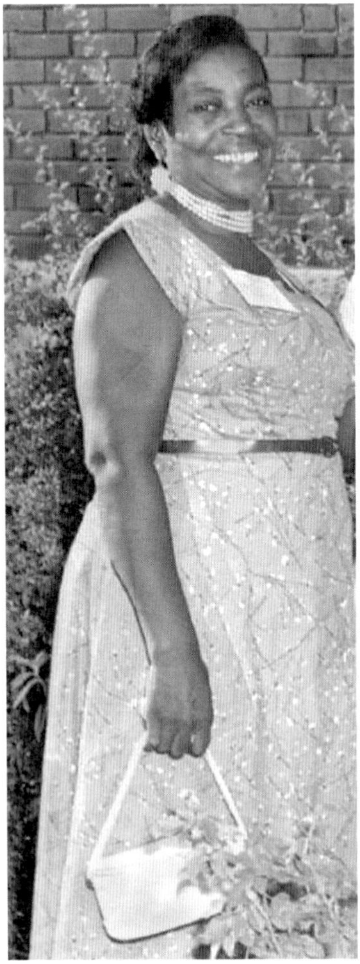

Celester Cole Hinton, Faye's grandmother and originator of the cheese butter rolls. *Courtesy Faye Hinton Futch.*

addition to the frogmore stew, they hold barbecues and fish fries. The fish—catfish, buffalo fish, brim and crappie—are all fried in big wash pots. Hush puppies and sides like Faye's famous coleslaw accompany the meals. They recently heard of a man near Palestine in St. Francis County who sold dressed pigs for pig roasts. The men prepared a fire pit in the backyard by digging a hole and then placing a large tractor tire rim over the top, with a couple of jack stands and a rod to act as a spit for the pig. Then they started their fire. The pig, which the women had soaked all night in a large tub filled with vinegar, salt and rosemary, was placed over the coals once they were ready. The men roasted the pig all night, drinking beer and enjoying one another's company. Once they were finished, around 4:00 a.m., they wrapped the pig in aluminum foil and left it on the grill covered until the women could work on the meat come morning. Someone brought some boudin sausage, venison steaks and several dressed squirrels to the event that were prepped and placed on the grill. The men ate the squirrels straight from the grill without any of them getting to the table.

GRANDMA CELESTER'S CHEESE BUTTER ROLLS

This is Grandmother Celester Hinton's wonderful cheese butter roll recipe, adapted to modern biscuits and not the ones made from the buttermilk. If you are not a fan of cheese, leave it out and just make yourself some plain ones. Be warned, though: once you have had them, you will not be happy until you have them again.

2 cups plain flour
pinch of salt
4 tablespoons cold water
(possibly a little more to get consistency you want)
nutmeg
1 stick butter, plus 2 tablespoons
2 tablespoons sugar, plus more to taste
½ cup grated cheese
⅓ cup Crisco shortening
1 can Carnation milk
water, to dilute the milk

Mix the flour, salt and water the same as pie crust. Make six balls with dough and roll out in round shapes. Next, sprinkle nutmeg, two tablespoons of butter and sugar to your taste) over the circles. Then sprinkle grated cheese (about ½ cup) and roll dough. Place the dough rolls in a casserole dish prepared with shortening. Next, boil 1 can of Carnation milk diluted with water, sugar, one stick of butter and about 1 teaspoon of nutmeg for about 5 to 10 minutes. Pour over the dough and bake in oven until the custard is thick and golden brown. Bake at 350°F.

CHAPTER 11
THE FUTURE OF DELTA FOOD

Arkansas remains a largely rural, agriculturally dependent state. According to the Arkansas Farm Bureau, 95 percent of the state's land is either in agriculture or devoted to forestry, bringing nearly $16 billion into the state's economy annually. Farming is still a big deal and nowhere more so than in the Delta. Although Arkansas is the leading rice-producing state in the nation, with Poinsett County at the top in production, cotton is still the main cash crop. Large-scale farming is the norm in the area, with most farmers working land that is rented from the large landowners, many of whom have controlled production for a century.

In a state where the average farm family works no more than forty acres, many of the small landholders have tired of the increasing cost of production and the need to farm more and more acres of land they do not own; there have been a few who have decided to go a different route. Specialty crops and value-added agriculture has been making an appearance in the Delta for the past decade. Those whose holdings are small are converting to specialized operations like crawfish ponds to keep the land in the family and in production. Honey production is on the rise, with many producers renting their hives to the larger farmers who produce crops like soybeans. The bees help with pollination and increased yields and in return convert the pollen into honey. Peace Farm at Proctor in Crittenden County started its farm in 1950, farming traditional crops like cotton and soybeans. In 2003, it was renamed Peace Bee Farm after the hobby hives morphed into well over one hundred. It sells primarily in the local region but will ship anywhere.

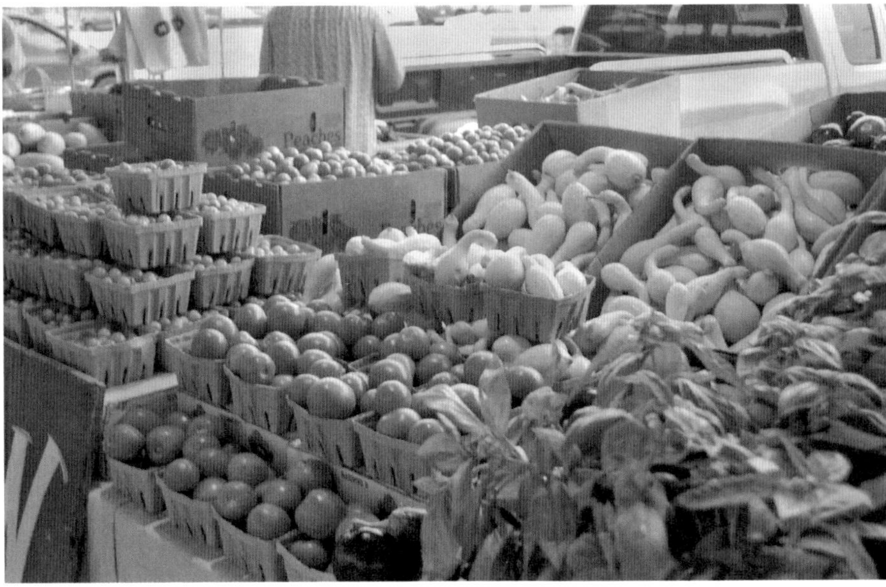

Whitton Farms stand at the Memphis Farmers' Market. *Courtesy Jill Forrester at Whitton Farms.*

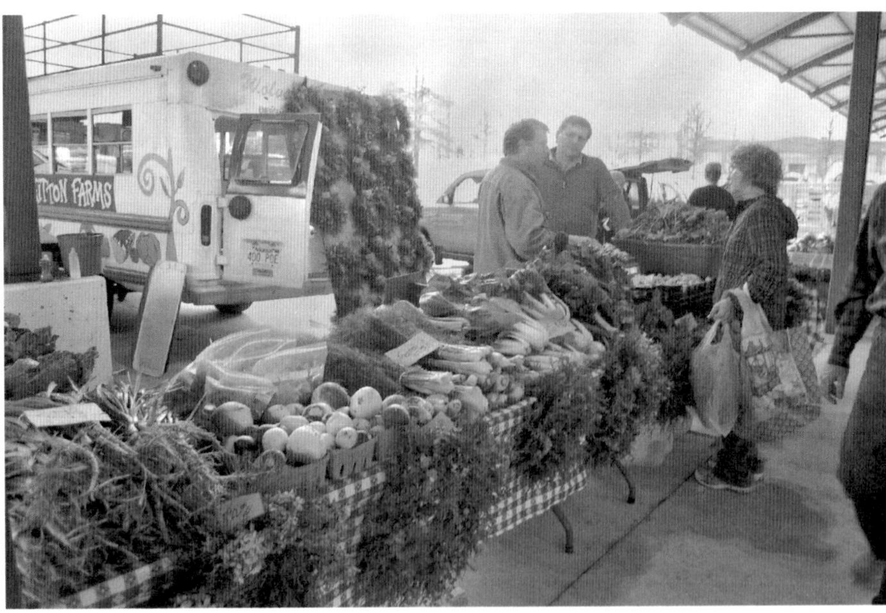

Keith Forrester (left) visits with customers at the farmers market. *Courtesy Jill Forrester at Whitton Farms.*

There are several niche operations in the region that serve a specialty market. Della Rice is a micro-milled rice grown in Brinkley, Monroe County, and is available in stores across the nation. Southern Brown Rice is an organically grown brown rice produced near Weiner in Poinsett County. Matthews Sweet Potato Farm has been in business for more than one hundred years and still going strong at Wynne in Cross County. One of the most unusual ventures in the Delta is Kona Cloud Coffee of Jonesboro. The coffee is actually grown on a farm in Hawaii and, once harvested, begins the processing route in Hawaii, but once the milling process and grading is finished, the coffee is bagged and shipped to Jonesboro for storage and roasting, which takes place in small batches to ensure freshness and quality.

Realizing that young people are more and more distant from the source of their food, even in an agricultural region like the Arkansas Delta, the Jonesboro School District as a part of the curriculum at its Health, Wellness and Environmental Studies Magnet Elementary School has a greenhouse and vegetable garden, and the students are learning to prepare in the kitchen the vegetables that they grow. Harrisburg Middle School, working with Arkansas Children's Hospital's Delta Garden Study, has also created a one-acre vegetable garden, as well as a chicken coop. It has a full-time garden manager to oversee the project. The project aims to reduce childhood obesity by teaching healthy eating habits, food preparation and increasing physical activity. The students learn how to build raised beds, test soil, compost and plant and harvest their crops.

Arkansas, like many other southern states, struggles with obesity. Although the traditional diet is heavy in vegetables, changes in lifestyle that include too much fast food and an overall lack of physical exercise have contributed to the problem. While the traditional ways of cooking in the South have been heavy on fats—even in vegetables, where salt pork or bacon has been the primary seasoning—perhaps a return to those foods will have a positive impact on the future. One positive step has been the growth of small farms like Keith and Jill Forrester's Whitton Farms in southern Mississippi County. They have not only made an impact locally but have also been featured in magazines and on television shows such as the PBS show *Endless Feast*. They are the future of Delta food.

If You Know Your Farmer, You Know Your Food: Whitton Farms

Jill Forrester loves flowers, so much so that in 2004 she convinced her husband to plow the old abandoned pastureland across the road from their rural Mississippi County home and plant a few pounds of sunflowers and zinnias for her birthday. Husband Keith is an obliging sort, so he did as asked. The fertile Delta soil produced a bumper crop, and after filling their home and the homes of everyone they knew with fresh bouquets, she loaded the car with buckets of cut flowers and headed out to the Memphis Farmers' Market one Saturday morning. By the end of the day, the car was empty and she had $400 in her pocket. From those humble beginnings, Whitton Farms was born.

The Forresters live and work on the family's six-hundred-acre farm in the tiny community of Whitton, Mississippi County. Keith grew up on the farm, and although he majored in education at Arkansas State University, his love of farming led him to the Peace Corps, where he worked as a sustainable agriculture volunteer in Lesotho/South Africa for two years. He returned home to Arkansas in 1998 and began teaching junior high health and coaching at Rivercrest Jr. and Sr. High School. He met Jonesboro native Jill, who was teaching junior high algebra, and they married in 2001. In 2002, they moved into his grandparents' house at Whitton and started growing vegetables for their own table. With Jill's success at the farmers' market, he expanded his vegetable gardens and added those to the flowers the following year. The couple now farm about twenty acres of flowers, herbs, vegetables, fruit and mushrooms on abandoned pastureland formerly grazed by his grandfather's prize horses.

Their success with the Memphis Farmers' Market led them to branch out to other farmers' markets, including the ASU Farmers' Market in Jonesboro, and they began delivering fresh produce to several local Memphis restaurants. Looking for a way to spread the risk as well as the profit, they next ventured into Community Supported Agriculture, more commonly known as a CSA. With the CSA model, local families pay a set amount

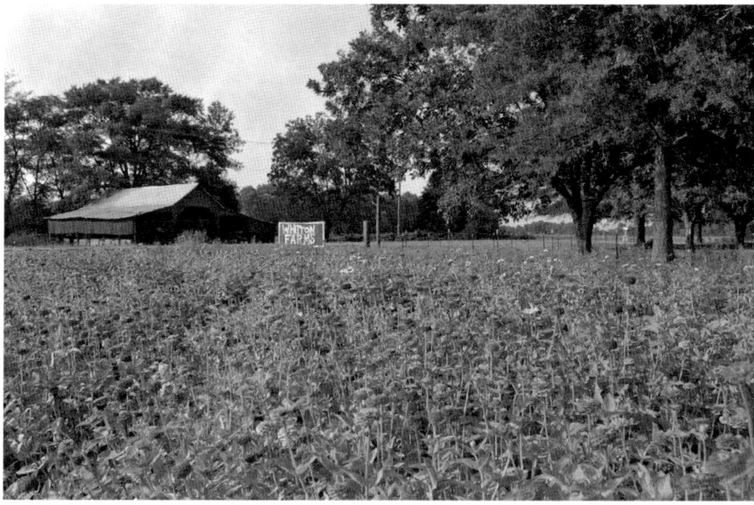

A field of zinnias at Whitton Farms. *Courtesy Jill Forrester at Whitton Farms.*

of money in the spring to help fund the purchase of seed and supplies. Throughout the season, they are rewarded with boxes of fresh farm produce every week. The risk factor comes from the uncertainty of farming. If there is not much rain or a later season frost, then the payoff for the CSA member families may not be as good, but if the weather cooperates and things go as planned, they can expect a bounty of produce every week. Jill likes utilizing the CSA not only because of the economic advantage that it provides for the farm but also because it allows her to introduce new varieties of produce to her customers. As a CSA member, you get a box of whatever is in season, so trying new things is one of the hazards associated with membership.

With the farm still producing more than they could sell fresh or through the CSA, they began looking for a way to take the farm to the city. They found a 6,400-square-foot building in midtown Memphis in the medical district along the city's trolley line that had formerly housed a night club and began the work to turn it into a fresh market serving not only Whitton Farms products but also those of other local producers from the region that includes Mississippi, Tennessee and Arkansas. The facility

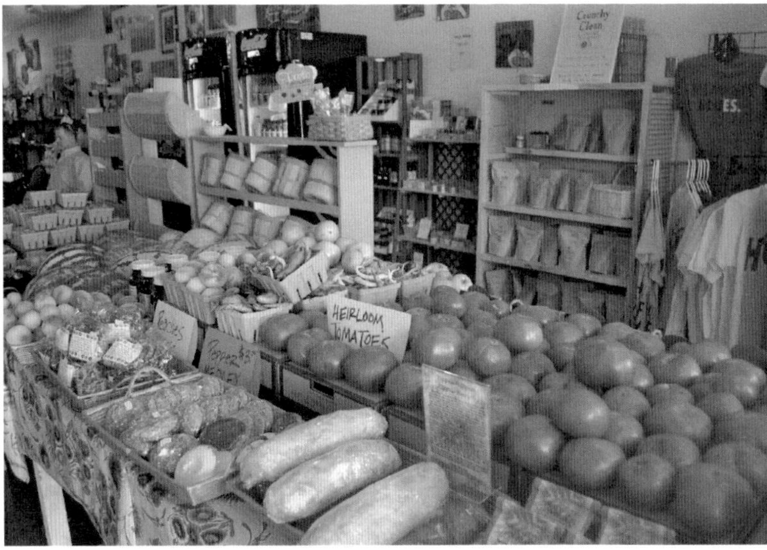

Fresh local produce, artisan breads and locally produced items at the Trolley Stop Market in Memphis, Tennessee, one of two farm-to-table restaurants and fresh markets operated by Whitton Farms. *Courtesy Jill Forrester at Whitton Farms.*

had a kitchen, so they decided to include a small deli, and after four months of remodeling, the Trolley Stop Market opened for business in 2010. They serve breakfast, lunch and dinner; cater and host events; and feature music on Friday nights. The business has been an overwhelming success and is one of Memphis's best-known farm-to-table restaurants. One of the features of the Trolley Stop is a pizza oven where the chefs try out some new fresh combinations in what is known as Jillbilly Pizza. The Potato Rosemary Pizza is their most popular item, but new creations are always in the works.

The success of Trolley Stop Market still did not take care of the abundance of produce that their farm provides, and in 2012, they founded the Whitton Farms Cannery at the farm, a full-service, USDA-certified commercial kitchen where they can develop a line of food products such as pickled okra and hot and spicy pickles, as well as rent the kitchen to other local food producers that need a commercial kitchen to create their products. Jill also realized that the art of home canning, which sustained many Delta families in the past, was being lost and has hosted home canning classes to teach others how to preserve their own produce.

Their success in taking the farm to the city with the Trolley Stop Market encouraged them to try bringing a bit of the city to the country. They have purchased the old Tyronza Grocery building in downtown Tyronza and are in the process of turning the place into a restaurant and fresh market in the country. To be known as Tyboogie's Café, it will lean more toward country-style foods served buffet style. Growing up in Jonesboro, Jill remembered that there was a favorite old restaurant that served a buffet and always had several vegetable options. She said that as a child, she was mesmerized by all of those vegetables and wants Tyboogie's to operate in the same way: good, safe, locally grown produce cooked the day it was picked in most cases. The menu will also feature pizza and sandwiches. She also hopes to include an ice cream counter because she has always wanted one. Keith is a barbecue guy, and he envisions adding it to the menu. Jill said that Keith loves smoked turkey necks more than any other food, especially cooked with his beans. He wants the item served up with cornbread to be a staple on the new menu.

Like the Trolley Stop, Tyboogie's will also feature a fresh market for locally grown and produced products like honey, jams and jellies and will operate in consignment fashion. Tyronza is a town of fewer than eight hundred residents and is mainly a bedroom community lying halfway between Memphis and Jonesboro, so the market is small and Clara's Midway Café has been in business for years. Jill hopes that Tyboogie's will be "the heart of Tyronza" and does not look at competing with Clara as much as promoting each other and the other little businesses that are beginning to pop up in the town.

Keith and Jill attribute their success to staying ahead of the market. They were primarily responsible for introducing heirloom vegetables to Memphis kitchens and have experimented extensively, looking for varieties that will handle the Delta heat and humidity. Because of their success with vegetables, they have moved into fruit production, adding blackberries, which Jill said "you can't kill" in the rich gumbo soil, and have installed an orchard of Arkansas Black apples that is doing well.

The future looks bright for Whitton Farm and the Forrester family. They have added the next generation to work the farm with the birth of their son, Fox. He has already shown an aptitude for the outdoors, building a stick collection that sits in a basket on a bookshelf in the house. They may have a budding horticulturalist on their hands. Only time will tell.

APPENDIX

I have mentioned many different plants, foods and producers in this volume. If you are interested in visiting any of the people I have talked to or want to visit their place of business, here is where you find the contact information. This is in no way a list of all the wonderful people and places you will want to visit. If you are in Marked Tree, look up my buddy Soozi Williams, who was supposed to be my coauthor on this book and is a fine Delta cook. A medical emergency put an end to her helping on the book and almost put an end to her. She was there in spirit, though, and I could not have done it without her guidance.

Restaurants

The Feed Lot
103 East State Street
Caraway, AR 72419
(870) 956-0055

Clara's Midway Café
153 North Main Street
Tyronza, AR 72386
(870) 487-2090

Atkins City Café
101 East Parkin Street
Parkin, AR 72373
(870) 755-2266

The Trolley Stop Market
704 Madison Avenue
Memphis, TN 38103
(901) 526-1361
www.trolleystopmarket.com

Tyboogie's Café
101 North Main Street
Tyronza, AR 72386
(870) 815-9519
www.facebook.com/TyboogiesCafe

The Dixie Pig
701 North Sixth Street
Blytheville, AR 72315
(870) 763-4636

The Kreme Kastle
121 North Division Street
Blytheville, AR 72315
(870) 762-2366

Johnson's Freeze Inn (Big Johnson's)
223 U.S. Highway 64
Wynne, AR 72396
(870) 238-3371

Little Johnson's Barbeque
310 Union Avenue
Wynne, AR 72396
(870) 208-8132

Johnson's Fish House and Diner
329 Highway 64 East
Wynne, AR 72396
(870) 238-3536

Woody's Barbeque
Corner of U.S. Highway 49 and Arkansas Route 14
Waldenburg, AR
(870) 579-2251
www.buywoodyssauce.com
Open Wednesday, Thursday and Friday

Bill Teague's Grocery
Highway 463
Trumann, AR 72472
(870) 483-5078

FOOD PRODUCERS

Granny Clay Homemade Foods
Marked Tree, AR
(870) 358-3708
Producer of chocolate gravy mix and hot pepper jelly

River City Spice Company
125 East Ash
Blytheville, AR 72316
(870) 763-6392
Producer of marinades, seasoning mixes, rubs and sauces

Whitton Farms
5157 West State Highway 118
Tyronza, AR 72386
(870) 815-9519
www.whittonfarms.com
Vegetables, fruits, mushrooms, relishes, jellies and pickles

Southern Brown Rice
8553 Rayburn Road
Weiner, AR 72479
(870) 684-2354
Certified organic white or brown basmati rice

Specialty Rice Inc.
1000 West First Street
Brinkley, AR 72021
1-800-467-1233 (toll free)
www.dellarice.com
Verified non-GMO arborio, jasmine and white and brown basmati rice

Matthews Ridgeview Farms
2400 Bartlett Road
PO Box 67
Wynne, AR 72396
(870) 238-8828
www.arsweetpotatoes.com

Delta Crawfish Market
4660 Highway 412 East
Paragould, AR 72450
(870) 335-2555
www.deltacrawfish.com

OTHER POINTS OF INTEREST

Widner-Magers Farm
Arkansas Highway 181 North
Dell, AR
www.widner-magers.org
Depression-era living history farm. You can also follow Dru at her "Country Farm Home" blog, www.thecountryfarmhome.blogspot.com.

Arkansas DeltaMade
www.arkansasdeltamade.com
A selection of products and services created and produced in the Arkansas Delta. The website features producers, retailers and contact information.

NOTES

Chapter 1

1. Dickens, *American Notes*, 109.
2. Cohn, *God Shakes Creation*, 14.
3. For a full look at this part of the Delta, see Cobb, *Most Southern Place on Earth*. It is the seminal work on the Yazoo-Mississippi Delta region and makes for fascinating reading. Percy's *Lanterns on the Levee* is an excellent read to experience the Delta through the eyes of one of the elite. For a look at the life of Shelby Foote and his early years in Greenville, see Chapman, *Shelby Foote*.
4. Longnecker, "A Road Divided," 208.
5. Cobb, *Most Southern Place on Earth*, 6.

Chapter 2

6. See Grisham, *Painted House*. Grisham is a native of northeast Arkansas; born in Jonesboro, he spent the first years of his life near Black Oak in Craighead County, which is also the setting of this novel. Hallmark Hall of Fame turned the book into a movie, which was filmed in two locations in northeast Arkansas. The farm scenes were filmed near

Clarkedale in Crittenden County and the town scenes at Lepanto in Poinsett County. The farmhouse that the movie company constructed for the Chandler family was presented to the City of Lepanto and has been reconstructed there at the southern edge of town on Arkansas Highway 135. It is operated as a museum of Delta life and is open by appointment only.

7. Arkansas DeltaMade is a marketing group originally created by the Rural Heritage Development Imitative and funded by a grant from the Kellogg Foundation. It promotes artisans, crafts persons and producers within the fifteen-county Arkansas Delta Byways tourism organization.
8. Soltow, *Men and Wealth*, 166.
9. See Clayton, Knight Jr. and Moore, *De Soto Chronicles*. This is a two-volume set that covers the entire expedition from start to finish and contains all of the translations of each of the chroniclers.
10. See Hudson, *Knights of Spain*. Hudson is an anthropologist who provides the best overview of the expedition in my opinion. He set out to retrace the route of the expedition with his wife, fellow anthropologist Joyce Rockwood Hudson, in 1984. She kept a journal of their trip that she later published (*Looking for De Soto*, 1993). It is also an excellent read and looks at the changes in the land and the people.
11. Arkansas Post was founded by Henri de Tonti at the site of a Quapaw village called Osotuoy, near the place where the Arkansas River enters the Mississippi River, although its location has moved several times over the years due to flooding. It is not only the location of the first semipermanent European settlement in the lower Mississippi Valley but was also the site of a Revolutionary War skirmish in 1783, the first territorial capital of Arkansas (1819–21) and the site of the Civil War Battle of Fort Hindman in 1863. The location is now a national monument.
12. Dougan, "Food and Foodways."
13. For more on the expedition into Arkansas, see Dunbar, *Forgotten Expedition*.
14. Interesting information about the earthquakes and their effects on not only the immediate region but also the rest of the nation can be found in Feldman, *When the Mississippi Ran Backwards*.
15. These two fascinating works are both available today. Featherstonhaugh's work is in two volumes, the Arkansas portion beginning the second volume, but both contain fascinating history, geology and geography of the United States in the early nineteenth century. Palmer's journal has been published by Arkansas Archeological Survey station archaeologist, Marvin Jeter, along with essays and notes on Palmer's findings and travels.

See Featherstonhaugh, *Excursion Through the Slave States*, and Jeter, *Edward Palmer's Arkansaw Mounds*.

16. The best general history of Arkansas, for those who want to study it further, is Dougan, *Arkansas Odyssey*.

CHAPTER 3

17. Lomax, "The State of Arkansas, #167," 323.
18. For more on plant domestication in the central United States, see Smith, Cowen and Hoffman, *Rivers of Change*.
19. There are numerous sources on Three Sisters gardening in print and on the web. I recommend the Three Sisters site from Renee's Garden Seeds, a seed company that also produces a combination seed packet for those interested in Three Sisters gardening. It is a fun project, especially good for children as it not only teaches the importance of growing your own food but nutrition as well. It also makes a very attractive garden.

CHAPTER 4

20. Dougan, "Food and Foodways."
21. For more on Johnson's barbeque restaurants and their cooking methods, see the Southern Foodways Alliance's Arkansas Barbeque Trail website for an oral history interview with Carolyn Johnson in 2009.

CHAPTER 5

22. Schrock, "Traditional Arkansas Foodways," 193. See also McDonough, *Garden Sass*. Both books are excellent regarding traditional folkways and food traditions, although both lean heavily toward traditions in the Ozarks region of the state. Small subsistence farming was the norm there and is still heavily practiced, so there is more of an emphasis on the traditional forms there. Also, the sharecroppers of the Delta were usually kept busy with the business of growing cotton, which is labor intensive, and therefore

the traditional things like hominy making were more likely to go by the wayside, especially after World War I.

23. With the emphasis placed on genetically modified organisms and the farm-to-table movement in this country, there has been a renewed emphasis on seed saving and the use of heirloom seeds. The White Whippoorwill is available once again from companies like Baker Creek Heirloom Seeds in Missouri and from places like the University of Central Arkansas, where Dr. Brian Campbell has spearheaded an effort to save the old seeds of Arkansas and has organized seed swaps for the past few years.

CHAPTER 6

24. Jennifer Harbster, "A Sweet Potato History," "Inside Adam," Library of Congress blog, November 24, 2010, http://blogs.loc.gov/inside_adams/2010/11/a-sweet-potato-history.

25. Scarry and Reitz, "Changes in Foodways at the Parkin Site," 108. The plant remnants were found in the excavation known as Locus Four, which contained European artifacts from the De Soto expedition like the Clarksdale bell.

26. Dougan, *Arkansas Odyssey*, 369. Buffalo Island is not actually an island but rather a high patch of land in the Big Lake and northern Sunk Lands region in Craighead County. During high water, it technically would be an island.

27. For further information on Delta politics and agriculture, see Whayne, *New Plantation South*.

CHAPTER 7

28. See Owens, *Cracker Cookbook*.

29. Jeannie M. Whayne has written a scholarly account of the story of the Italian immigrants at Sunnyside called *Shadows Over Sunnyside*. Many members of the group left Sunnyside—led by their priest, Father Bandini—and headed for the Ozarks, where they settled and established Tontitown in Benton County in northwest Arkansas. A smaller group moved on to

central Missouri and established the community of Rosati, which is in the center of Missouri's grape growing and wine producing region.

30. John T. Edge, director of the Southern Foodways Alliance at the University of Mississippi, wrote his master's thesis on the argument, and it is a worthy read for those with an interest in food, history and politics.

CHAPTER 9

31. Bumpers, *Best Lawyer in a One Lawyer Town*, 245.

CHAPTER 10

32. For a good description of the hog killing process and the traditions associated with it, see Schrock, "Traditional Arkansas Foodways."

BIBLIOGRAPHY

Family Papers and Other Collections

Widner-Magers Papers, Dell, Arkansas family farm.

Newspapers

Arkansas Democrat.
Arkansas Gazette.
Jonesboro Sun.
Lepanto News Record.
Marked Tree Tribune.
Memphis Commercial-Appeal.
Osceola (AR) Times.
Parkin (AR) Free Press.
Parkin (AR) Times.
Poinsett County Democrat-Tribune.
Trumann Democrat.

INTERVIEWS AND CONVERSATIONS

Cantrell, Gertrude Marshall. Lepanto, Poinsett County, December 30, 1986.
Duncan, Dru. Dell, Mississippi County, December 16, 2012.
Forrester, Jill and Keith. Whitton, Mississippi County, December 17, 2012.
Futch, Faye Hinton. Parkin, Cross County, December 2, 2012.
Green, Clara Nell. Tyronza, Poinsett County, November 17, 2012.
Haynes, Marion. Yarbro, Mississippi County, January 18, 2013.
Lawrie, Danette Portis Watkins. Lepanto, Poinsett County, November 12, 2012.
Prestidge, Teddy. Tyronza, Poinsett County, March 21, 2008.
Staggs, Elise Anderson. Caraway, Craighead County, November 13, 2012.
Williams, Soozi. Marked Tree, Poinsett County, various dates.
Williams, Tom. Marked Tree, Poinsett County, various dates.

BOOKS AND PERIODICAL ARTICLES

American Cancer Society, Arkansas Division. *Arkansas Heritage: Recipes Past and Present.* Nashville, TN: Favorite Recipes Press, 1992.

Arkansas Federation of Women's Clubs. *Treats from Arkansas Kitchens.* Malvern, AR: self-published, 1965.

Arnold, Morris S. *Colonial Arkansas, 1686–1804: A Social and Cultural History.* Fayetteville: University of Arkansas Press, 1991.

Ashley, Liza. *Thirty Years at the Mansion.* Little Rock, AR: August House, 1985.

Ayers, Edward L. *Southern Crossing: A History of the American South, 1877–1906.* New York: Oxford University Press, 1998.

Bailey, Garrick. "Continuity and Change in Mississippian Civilization." *Hero, Hawk, and Open Hand: American Indian Art of the Ancient Midwest and South.* Edited by Richard Townsend. New Haven, CT: Yale University Press, 2004.

Bolsterli, Margaret Jones. *Born in the Delta: Reflections on the Making of a Southern White Sensibility.* Fayetteville: University of Arkansas, 2002.

———. *During Wind and Rain: The Jones Family Farm in the Arkansas Delta, 1848–2006.* Fayetteville: University of Arkansas Press, 2008.

———. *Vinegar Pie and Chicken Bread: A Woman's Diary of Life in the Rural South, 1890–1891.* Fayetteville: University of Arkansas Press, 1982.

Bower, Anne L., ed. *Recipes for Reading: Community Cookbooks, Stories, Histories.* Amherst: University of Massachusetts Press, 1997.

Brothwell, Don, and Patricia Brothwell. *Food in Antiquity: A Survey of the Diet of the Early Peoples.* Baltimore, MD: Johns Hopkins University Press, 1969.

Bumpers, Dale. *The Best Lawyer in a One Lawyer Town: A Memoir.* Fayetteville: University of Arkansas Press, 2004.

Chapman, C. Stuart. *Shelby Foote: A Writer's Life.* Oxford: University of Mississippi Press, 2006.

Clayton, Lawrence A., Vernon James Knight Jr. and Edward C. Moore, eds. *The De Soto Chronicles: The Expedition of Hernando de Soto to North America in 1539–1543.* Vol. 1. Tuscaloosa: University of Alabama Press, 1993.

Cobb, James C. *The Most Southern Place on Earth: The Mississippi Delta and the Roots of Regional Identity.* New York: Oxford University Press, 1992.

———. *The South and America Since World War II.* New York: Oxford University Press, 2011.

Cohn, David L. *God Shakes Creation.* New York: Harper Brothers, 1938.

Coulter, Lynn. *Gardening with Heirloom Seeds: Tried-and-True Flowers, Fruits and Vegetables for a New Generation.* Chapel Hill: University of North Carolina Press, 2006.

Cox, Beverly, and Martin Jacobs. *Spirit of the Harvest: North American Indian Cooking.* New York: Stewart, Tabori and Chang, 1991.

Danbom, David B. *Born in the Country: A History of Rural America.* Baltimore, MD: Johns Hopkins University Press, 1995.

Daniel, Pete. *Lost Revolutions: The South in the 1950s.* Chapel Hill: University of North Carolina Press, 2000.

Daniels, Jonathan. *A Southerner Discovers the South.* New York: DeCapo Press, 1970.

Dickens, Charles. *American Notes for General Circulation.* Vol. 2. London: Chapman and Hall, 1842.

Dougan, Michael B. *Arkansas Odyssey: The Saga of Arkansas from Prehistoric Times to the Present.* Little Rock, AR: Rose Publishing Company, 1994.

———. "Food and Foodways." *The Arkansas Encyclopedia of History and Culture.* Little Rock: Central Arkansas Library System, 2013.

Dragonwagon, Crescent. *The Cornbread Gospels.* New York: Workman Publishing, 2007.

Dunbar, William. *The Forgotten Expedition, 1804–1805: The Louisiana Purchase Journals of Dunbar and Hunter.* Edited by Trey Berry, Pam Beasley and Jeanne Clements. Baton Rouge: Louisiana State University Press, 2006.

East, Charles. "The Delta." *Place in American Fiction: Excursions and Explorations.* Edited by H.L. Weatherby and George Core. Columbia: University of Missouri Press, 2004.

Edge, John T. *Fried Chicken: An American Story.* New York: G.P. Putnam's Sons, 2004.

———. *A Gracious Plenty: Recipes and Recollections from the American South.* New York: HP Books, 1999.

———. "In through the Back Door." *Oxford American*, March 22, 2010.

———. *Southern Belly: The Ultimate Food Lovers' Companion to the South.* Athens, GA: Hill Street Press, 2000.

Edrington, Mabel F. *History of Mississippi County, Arkansas.* Ocala, FL: Ocala Star-Banner, 1962.

Egerton, John, ed. *Cornbread Nation I: The Best of Southern Food Writing.* Chapel Hill: University of North Carolina Press, 2002.

Ellenberg, George B. *Mule South to Tractor South: Mules, Machines and the Transformation of the Cotton South.* Tuscaloosa: University of Alabama Press, 2007.

Fagan, Brian. *The Little Ice Age: How Climate Made History, 1300–1850.* New York: Basic Books, 2000.

Featherstonhaugh, G.W. *Excursion through the Slave States, from Washington on the Potomac to the Frontier of Mexico.* Vol. 2. Cambridge, MA: Cambridge University Press, 2011.

Feldman, Jay. *When the Mississippi Ran Backwards: Empire, Intrigue, Murder, and the New Madrid Earthquakes of 1811–1812.* New York: Free Press, 2005.

Ferris, Marcie Cohen. *Matzoh Ball Gumbo: Culinary Tales of the Jewish South.* Chapel Hill: University of North Carolina Press, 2005.

Foster, Sara. *Sara Foster's Southern Kitchen: Soulful, Traditional, Seasonal.* New York: Random House, 2011.

Gatewood, Willard B. "The Arkansas Delta: Deepest of the Deep South." *The Arkansas Delta: Land of Paradox.* Edited by Jeannie M. Whayne and Carl H. Moneyhon. Fayetteville: University of Arkansas Press, 1993.

Grisham, Cindy L. "When Hope Grows Weary: An Arkansas Delta Town in Space and Place." PhD diss., Arkansas State University, 2012.

Grisham, John. *A Painted House.* New York: Doubleday, 2001.

Hamilton, Mary. *Trials of the Earth: The Autobiography of Mary Hamilton.* Edited by Helen Dick Davis. Jackson: University Press of Mississippi, 1992.

Hill, Elizabeth Griffin. *A Splendid Piece of Work, 1912–2012: One Hundred Years of Arkansas Home Demonstration and Extension Homemakers Clubs.* Little Rock, AR: self-published, 2012.

Hooks, Bell. *Belonging: A Culture of Place.* New York: Routledge, 2009.

Hudson, Charles. *Knights of Spain, Warriors of the Sun: Hernando de Soto and the South's Ancient Chiefdoms.* Athens: University of Georgia Press, 1997.

Hudson, Joyce Rockwood. *Looking for De Soto: A Search through the South for the Spaniard's Trail.* Athens, GA: University of Georgia Press, 1993.

Jeter, Marvin D., ed. *Edward Palmer's Arkansaw Mounds.* Fayetteville: University of Arkansas Press, 1990.

Johnson, Clifton. *Highway and Byways of the Mississippi Valley.* Maclachan Bell Press, 2008.

Kurlansky, Mark. *The Food of a Younger Land: A Portrait of American Food—Before the National Highway System, Before Chain Restaurants, and Before Frozen Food, When the Nation's Food Was Seasonal, Regional, and Traditional—From the Lost WPA Files.* New York: Riverhead Books, 2010.

Lemann, Nicholas. *The Promised Land: The Great Black Migration and How It Changed America.* New York: A.A. Knopf, 1991.

LeMaster, Carolyn Gray. *A Corner of the Tapestry: A History of the Jewish Experience in Arkansas, 1820–1990.* Fayetteville: University of Arkansas Press, 1994.

Lomax, Alan, comp. "The State of Arkansas." No. 167 in *The Folksongs of North America: In the English Language.* New York: Doubleday, 1960.

Longnecker, Julia Ward. "A Road Divided: From Memphis to Little Rock through the Great Mississippi Swamp." *Arkansas Historical Quarterly* 44, no. 3 (Autumn 1985): 208.

Lundy, Ronni, ed. *Cornbread Nation III: Foods of the Mountain South.* Chapel Hill: University of North Carolina Press, 2005.

Mann, Charles C. *1491: New Revelations of the Americas Before Columbus.* New York: Vintage Books, 2005.

———. *1493: Uncovering the New World Columbus Created.* New York: Alfred A. Knopf, 2011.

Marked Tree Historical Society. *The Museum Cookbook.* Adamsville, TN: Keepsake Cookbooks, 1996.

Marvell Academy Mother's Association. *High Cotton Cookin'.* Memphis, TN: Wimmer Brothers Press, 1978.

McDonough, Nancy. *Garden Sass: A Catalog of Arkansas Folkways.* New York: Coward, McCann & Georghagan, 1975.

McMath, Phillip H. *Lost Kingdoms.* Fayetteville, AR: Phoenix International Inc., 2007.

McNeil, William K., and William M. Clements, eds. *An Arkansas Folklore Sourcebook.* Fayetteville: University of Arkansas Press, 1992.

Metcalf, Gayden, and Charlotte Hays. *Being Dead Is No Excuse: The Official Southern Ladies Guide to Hosting the Perfect Funeral.* New York: Miramax Books, 2005.

Moneyhon, Carl H. *Arkansas and the New South, 1874–1929.* Fayetteville: University of Arkansas Press, 1997.

———. "Delta Towns: Their Rise and Decline." *The Arkansas Delta: Land of Paradox*. Edited by Jeannie M. Whayne and Carl H. Moneyhon. Fayetteville: University of Arkansas Press, 1993.

Morse, Phyllis A. *Parkin: The 1978–1979 Archeological Investigations of a Cross County, Arkansas Site*. Fayetteville: Arkansas Archeological Survey, 1981.

Nabhan, Gary Paul, ed. *Renewing America's Food Traditions: Saving and Savoring the Continent's Most Endangered Foods*. White River Junction, VT: Chelsea Green Publishing Company, 2008.

Oldenburg, Ray. *The Great Good Place: Cafes, Coffee Shops, Bookstores, Bars, Hair Salons, and Other Hangouts at the Heart of a Community*. Cambridge, MA: DaCapo Press, 1997.

Otto, John Solomon. *The Final Frontier, 1880–1930: Settling the Southern Bottomlands*. Westport, CT: Greenwood Press, 1999.

Owens, Janis. *The Cracker Cookbook: A Cookbook in Celebration of Cornbread-Fed, Down-Home Family Stories and Cuisine*. New York: Scribner, 2009.

Percy, William Alexander. *Lanterns on the Levee: Recollections of a Planter's Son*. Library of Southern Civilization Series. Baton Rouge: Louisiana State University Press, 2006.

Reed, Dale Volberg, and John Shelton Reed, eds. *Cornbread Nation IV: The Best of Southern Food Writing*. Athens: University of Georgia Press, 2008.

Reed, John Shelton. *Minding the South*. Columbia: University of Missouri Press, 2003.

Reed, Julia. *Queen of the Turtle Derby and Other Southern Phenomena*. New York: Random House, 2004.

Ritter, Anna. "Marked Tree from 1883–1936." *Marked Tree Tribune*, July 17, 1939.

Scarry, C. Margaret, and Elizabeth J. Reitz. "Changes in Foodways at the Parkin Site, Arkansas." *Southeastern Archaeology* 24, no. 2 (Winter 2005): 107–20.

Schenone, Laura. *A Thousand Years Over a Hot Stove: A History of American Women Told through Food, Recipes, and Remembrances*. New York: W.W. Norton, 2003.

Schrock, Earl F., Jr. "Traditional Arkansas Foodways." *An Arkansas Folklore Sourcebook*. Edited by W.K. McNeil and William M. Clements. Fayetteville: University of Arkansas Press, 1992.

Smith, Art. *Back to the Table: The Reunion of Food and Family*. New York: Hyperion, 2001.

Smith, Bruce D. "Agricultural Chiefdoms of the Eastern Woodlands." *The Cambridge History of the Native Peoples of the Americas*. Vol. 1, *North America*. Edited by Bruce G. Trigger and Wilcomb E. Washburn. New York: Cambridge University Press, 1996.

Smith, Bruce D., C. Wesley Cowen and Michael P. Hoffman. *Rivers of Change: Essays on Early Agriculture in Eastern North America.* Tuscaloosa: University of Alabama Press, 1992.

Smith, C. Calvin. *War and Wartime Changes: The Transformation of Arkansas, 1940–1945.* Fayetteville: University of Arkansas Press, 1986.

Soltow, Lee. *Men and Wealth in the United States, 1850–1870.* New Haven, CT: Yale University Press, 1975.

The Southern Heritage Cookbook. Birmingham, AL: Oxmoor House, 1983.

Swank, Roy. *Trail to Marked Tree.* San Antonio, TX: Naylor Company, 1968.

Theophano, Janet. *Eat My Words: Reading Women's Lives through the Cookbooks They Wrote.* New York: Palgrave MacMillian, 2002.

Von Hesse-Wartegg, Ernst. *Travels on the Lower Mississippi, 1879–1880: A Memoir by Ernst von Hesse-Wartegg.* Edited by Frederic Trautmann. Columbia: University of Missouri Press, 1990.

Wallace, Henry A. *Corn and Corn Growing.* New York: John Wiley and Sons Inc., 1937.

Whayne, Jeannie M. "Creation of a Plantation System in the Arkansas: Delta in the Twentieth Century." *Agricultural History* 66, no. 1 (Winter 1992): 63–84.

———. *A New Plantation South: Land, Labor, and Federal Favor in Twentieth Century Arkansas.* Charlottesville: University Press of Virginia, 1996.

———. "Robert E. Lee Wilson and the Making of a Post-Civil War Plantation." *The Southern Elite and Social Change: Essays in Honor of Willard B. Gatewood Jr.* Edited by Randy Finley and Thomas A. DeBlack. Fayetteville: University of Arkansas Press, 2002.

Whayne, Jeannie M., and Willard B. Gatewood. *The Arkansas Delta: Land of Paradox.* Fayetteville: University of Arkansas Press, 1993.

Whitaker, Robert. *On the Laps of Gods: The Red Summer of 1919 and the Struggle for Justice that Remade a Nation.* New York: Crown Publishers, 2008.

Willard, Pat. *America Eats: On the Road with the WPA—The Fish Fries, Box Supper Socials, and Chitlin Feasts that Define Real American Food.* New York: Bloomsbury, 2008.

Winne, Mark. *Closing the Food Gap: Resetting the Table in the Land of Plenty.* Boston: Beacon Press, 2008.

Woodward, C. Vann. *The Burden of Southern History.* Baton Rouge: Louisiana State University Press, 1993.

———. *Origins of the New South, 1877–1913.* Baton Rouge: Louisiana State University Press, 1971.

Zimmer, Anne Carter. *The Robert E. Lee Family Cooking and Housekeeping Book.* Chapel Hill: University of North Carolina, 1997.

INDEX

ABOUT THE AUTHOR

Cindy Grisham loves eating and talking about food. She is a former police officer (you can rest assured that if police cars are parked outside a restaurant, it is a good place to eat) who grew weary of that line of work and went back to school to pursue a new career in history and heritage. She is a graduate of Missouri State University and Arkansas State University, where she received a PhD in heritage studies. She currently works as an independent historian and genealogist based in Benton, Arkansas, where she lives with her boys, Tim the man and Jack the dog.